Jesus The Man

How Jesus' Humanity Affects Our Identity

Jesus the Man

© Copyright 2019 by Carol Kidd

ISBN 978-1-950252-12-1

Jesus the Man

How Jesus' Humanity Affects Our Identity

By Carol Kidd

Dedication

To my dad, Lon DeNeff, who will probably never realize what a miracle he was in my life, and how much two little girls loved having a dad.

To my mom, Peggy Hickson, who started me on the greatest adventure of my life, by reading the Bible and Bible stories to me as I was growing up.

Acknowledgements

I would like to thank the Holy Spirit, for being on this planet with us. I wouldn't want to be here without you. And for teaching me the stuff in this book. And for helping me to pray.

I would like to thank my sister for encouraging me to write this book. Without her coaching, praise, encouragement and figuring out the process, I never would have gotten this written.

Thank you, Jesus the Man, your love is inconceivable. What you have done for us to bring us redemption is so amazing sometimes all I can do is cry.

Thank you, Father God, your imagination is magnificent.

Thank you, Lili, Violet and Joshua for helping with the computer, I love having computer geniuses in the house.

Thank you, Walter for being the best friend anyone could ever have.

Contents

Introduction

Ring, ring, my phone was ringing. "Who could be calling this early?" I asked myself. I answered.

"Summer!" I heard my twin sister's voice exclaim. Her voice was so overcome with emotion I could not tell if she were laughing or crying. For a second I felt alarm.

"Are you okay?" I asked.

She struggled to gain composure and then shouted, "Yes!" She struggled again, "God has been showing me something and it is so awesome!" Then Carol proceeded to tell me the incredible revelation she received in the night.

This happens to me. Carol has called before. And as I get ready for work and she gets kids off to school, she reveals to me the secrets and mysteries hidden in God's word that she has uncovered. As she tells me and explains those scriptures I have never understood before, I am filled with awe and wonder. She makes God bigger and bigger to me until my mind is blown and I feel a new sense of exhilaration. My mind has to stretch to understand what she is saying, but she explains it bit by bit in a way I can fathom.

She has always been smart. I was just looking at an old scrapbook the other day, and there were our report cards, I had a couple B's a couple C's and a D. She has A's with B+ and a B, probably in Gym class. She has an incredible mind, and her greatest thrill is to study God's word. As I hung up the phone and started to go to work, I had a new thrill surging through me. God was so much more awesome than I could possibly imagine. Carol's latest revelation had done what it always does, encouraged me, built up my faith and filled me with awe for God

This book is your ring, ring. Open it and hear my sister's words and let them build your faith and encourage you. And also let them fill you with wonder at the magnitude and beauty of our God.   -Summer McClellan

Chapter 1

The Pre-Incarnate Jesus Our Creator

In this book I would like to take a look at Jesus, our Savior, Redeemer, and so much more, and just examine Him as well as we can: who He is, what He has done for us, and what is our relationship with Him.

We are so familiar with Jesus, the baby in Bethlehem, the man with the disciples, Jesus on the cross, and even the resurrected Jesus, sometimes I wonder about the Jesus who existed eternally with the Father. We don't know much about what He was like then. John tells us He was the Word.

"In the beginning was the Word, and the Word was with God, and the Word was God. He was in the beginning with God. All things came into being through Him, and apart from Him nothing came into being that has come into being." John 1:1-3

That doesn't make a lot of sense. Is the Word a name or was He really the Word? Or does that describe His function in the Creation. I don't know. I do know that He was with God and He is God, He was The Word and that He created everything.

"God, after He spoke long ago to the fathers in the prophets in many portions and in many ways, in these last days has spoken to us in His Son, whom He appointed heir of all things, through whom also He made the world. And He is the radiance of His glory and the exact representation of His nature and upholds all things by the word of His power." Hebrews 1:1-3

The verse quoted above from the book of Hebrews also speaks of the Word of His Power upholding all things. We see from these verses that He is our Creator and the Sustainer of all matter.

Colossians 1:16-17 confirms this *"For by Him all things were created, both in the heavens and on earth, visible and invisible, whether thrones or dominions or rulers or authorities, all things have been created through Him and for Him. **He is before all things and in Him all things hold together."***

We seldom think about the impossibility of our own existence or the existence of the world around us. I love to think about true science, because when you think about it, science IS the study of God. How He made things. How He operates. Science is a peek into who that pre-incarnate Jesus was and who He is now. And often the physical principles of science help us understand how things work in the spirit realm. Even though the creation isn't the way it was before death entered the world, it is still His creation. What better way to learn about Him, His incredible genius, His mathematical precision, His omniscience, and even His sense of humor. We can do this. Romans 1:20 says *"For since the creation of the world, His invisible attributes, His eternal power and divine nature, have been clearly seen, being understood through what has been made."*

Science and Creation

We take for granted the world around us and our own bodies or existence. It is familiar and normal to us. I don't think we question it. But if we could step outside of the familiarity of the world around us or even the indoctrination of the so-called science we learned in school and look at things objectively, it is pretty impossible that anything at all exists. One thing we know is: it is impossible to make something from nothing. Scientist's with all their newfangled knowledge and machines can't do it. It is impossible. And yet here we are. What explanation can be made, for there is a whole lot of something and no logical explanation for how it got here.

The First Law of Thermodynamics

The first law of thermodynamics says that we live in a closed system. No new energy/matter can be added. (Solomon said it this way *"There is nothing new under the sun."*) Energy and matter are the same thing, in that sense, because matter is made of energy. There is nothing new. It is just transformed from one state to another. Hebrews 4:3 confirms this where it states, *"Although His works were finished from the foundation of the world."* God's works were finished from the foundation of the world. He then rested or stopped His work. It is all done. All the energy and creative power He exerted in those first six days are what the universe is running on now. He doesn't have to keep creating energy. It was finished. The energy and matter we have changes form, but no new energy or matter is created. Here is an example, the sun's energy grows grass, which feeds a cow, which we eat, which gives us the energy we need to work. The energy was transferred from the sun to the grass to the cow to us. Another example is how the water cycle works. It is the same water that has been around since creation. It falls and then evaporates, makes new clouds and falls again. The principle of energy is the same except some of it is lost as heat and not able to be recovered. So gradually there will be an end of the energy in our universe. Scientists call it "heat death". Science acknowledges that we have a set amount of matter/energy. But where did it come from. You still can't get something from nothing. Whatever you believe about creation, evolution, the Big Bang, aliens from other planets, or whatever other belief, you still have to come to that very beginning point and that is that something had to come from nothing. I believe God is the only answer.

11

Evolution

When I said true science is the study of God, I meant TRUE science. I do not believe evolution is science at all. I believe it is deception and even political manipulation, but not science. Dr. Kent Hovind has a series of videos you can watch free on YouTube that deals with the topic much better than I ever could. Evolution is contrary to the Second Law of Thermodynamics. A simple definition of this law is: *everything moves from order to chaos.* Just as the matter and energy are slowing running down as energy is lost. It seems order is being lost also. When God created everything, it was good. It is now moving toward decay, running down like the ticking of a watch. Think about if you left your house for five years and came back. Would you expect to find it in better or worse shape? How about twenty years? In a hundred years it would probably be a heap of rubble. Evolution is kind of like going to ancient ruins and expecting to find a modern city with electricity, running water and Wi-Fi. Evolution has the order backwards. Evolution has the universe moving from chaos to order, rather than order to chaos. Which seems pretty crazy and even then, it still can't explain the original dilemma. You just can't get something from nothing. God is the only explanation. The order, information and energy that God set into motion on those first six days is the order information and energy that runs the universe to this day. It is ticking down, but there was a beginning point.

That beginning point, that order, information and energy was God.

Some might say where did God come from? Well see, that is in the definition that makes Him God. He is God because He is preexistent and everything else exists because of Him. He is outside of and supersedes the creation itself. This is really the only logical explanation.

Someone outside of the universe, someone with an intelligence, scope, power and ability way beyond the human mind has to be responsible. Someone with the ability to make something from nothing.

Quantum Physics

The reason for writing about quantum physics is not really to learn about physics, so much as to learn about God. Science helps me to see Him more clearly. I love thinking about quantum physics. It helps me understand Bible concepts better. Quantum physics is really in opposition to evolution, but fits very well in to the principles of scripture. Unfortunately, many secular scientists have used new age philosophies and humanism to ignore God and His fingerprint in their discoveries.

What is quantum physics? It is the study of the tiniest building blocks of creation. Let's take our human body for example. We are made up of different organs. If you break those down you get cells. If you break the cells down you get molecules. When you break the molecules down, you get atoms. So far so good, everything still seems normal. But when you break atoms apart and study what they are made of, our whole concept of reality is suddenly changed. The laws of physics and our understanding of the nature of reality changes. We learn that nothing is as it appears.

Is A Solid, Solid?

What if I were to tell you that you are mostly empty space? You might react like I did. "That's impossible. I can feel myself. I'm solid."

What if I were to tell you that you are empty space. If equated in time, you would be solid to empty space the same ratio as one second would be to 30 million years? That is your solidness would be represented by one second. Your empty space would be represented by 30 million years. Sounds impossible. Our experience seems to tell us otherwise. Chuck Missler explains the details in an article entitled *Science and the Bible Part 1 The Nature of Our Reality.* "**The hydrogen atom is approximately 0.00000001 centimeters in diameter, usually abbreviated as (10)-8 cm. The nucleus consisting of a single proton is approximately .0000000000001 centimeters in diameter, usually abbreviated as (10)-13 cm. In linear terms that's a ratio of (10)-8/ (10)-13 which is (10)-5 or 100,000 times! That may be a bit too abstract for most of us. Let's try to picture making a "model" of this. Let's take a golf ball to represent the nucleus; our electron would have to be over a mile or 55 football fields away! But that's the linear differential. To represent this volumetrically (length x width x height), we need (10)5)3 or (10)15, a numerical relationship which is virtually impossible for us to grasp! It is the same relationship that one second has to 30 million years!**"[1]

Wow! That sure changes my concept of reality! Our whole concept of what is solid is wrong! We really live in an electrical simulation of solid material. Things are not solid at all!

There is a wonderful Moody Science video made in the 1960's, called *Facts of Faith*. I would highly recommend watching it. It is available today. In it, Doctor Irwin Moon talks about this very subject. "**Atoms are not solid instead they are tiny solar systems composed of infinitely small particles revolving at tremendous speeds and bound together by enormous forces. And like a solar system, atoms are almost entirely empty space... If I were to attempt to run through that wall right now, all I'd get for my trouble**

---

[1] Chuck Missler, "Science and the Bible, The Nature of our Reality", *Personal Update News Journal*, March 1, 2008, https: khouse.org/articles/2008/

would be a good-sized lump on the head. But that which would prevent my body passing through the wall would not be a collision of particles, but rather a collision of forces. The same forces that make an atom bomb. If it were not for these forces my body could go freely back and forth through that wall just as though it were not there."[2] Dr. Moon then goes on to explain it is scientifically possible for two worlds to coexist in the same place at the same time, passing freely through one another, without even being aware of the other. The only requirement being the atomic forces in each not being mutually interactive. (I believe this means at a different frequency.) He goes on to prove his statement. Dr. Moon has 1,000,000 volts of electricity pass through his body, without harm! Watching him perform this experiment is pretty unforgettable. My kids and I have watched this video several times. I think I learn more every time I watch it.

If you've never heard of this before, it is quite a lot to take in. My son and I like to talk about these things. I tell him, "You are not a boy, you are an electrical simulation of a boy."

If the atomic forces in your body were to suddenly release or stop (I think that would be the part that Jesus upholds with the word of His power!) we would have to find what was left (if indeed there is anything) with a microscope. Two worlds could (and do!) coexist. The physical and spiritual realm.

Our Eyes, Light Receptors

You might be thinking, yes, but if there were another world present, surely, I would be able to see it. Not necessarily, our senses are really just receptors that carry information to our brains. Light is particularly interesting to me, because I am somewhat of an artist. When you paint

[2] Moody Press *Facts of Faith* (Chicago, IL, Moody Publishers 2004)

or draw, you learn that what you are drawing or painting, (if you want it to look realistic) is not lines or solid colors, it is light. An artist looks at how the light is reflecting off of something and learns to put down on paper or canvas what they actually see, not what they think they see. Right now, I am looking at my green chair. I know it is green. If I were to paint it using my green paint only, it wouldn't look like anything. Looking at my chair across the room, the light is hitting it in spots that look almost completely white. In cracks and crevices, it looks almost black and much of my green chair looks gray.

When we look at an object, we are not seeing the object, in reality, we only can see light. Our eyes are light detectors. The chair does not make any contact to my eye. Light bounces off of the chair. The color I see is actually in the light, not in the chair. All you can see or will ever see is light rays. Your eyes are created to pick up a small spectrum of light. If you look at the entire spectrum of light waves, what we can see is a very small portion, .0035%! What if we could see more of the light spectrum? What would we see? Maybe that other dimension.

There is a video on YouTube of a group of Christians worshipping around a bonfire. Apparently, the darkness and the bonfire allowed the camera to pick up light rays outside of the scope of the natural human eye, because it picked up an angel dancing and worshipping around the fire with them! When I first found this video, I watched it over and over again. I know the spirit realm exists. I believe it. I know it. But here it was right in front of me. Wow! It was mind blowing to me. Even though I know it is true, to see it on video was awesome.   I don't think the presence of angels is a rare thing. Picking them up on camera is though! The days of you can only believe what you see are unscientific and outdated.

I had a strange experience that really brought this home to me.   I had a minor surgery and was given the choice of being totally under sedation or a spinal tap that took all feeling away from the bottom half of my body. I chose the latter. I suppose it isn't all that rare, but it was a very strange experience for me. I could not feel or move the lower half of my body. I was awake during the surgery, and then afterward I was returned to a room where my husband was. The nurse happened to be a friend of ours and she asked my husband to help change the bedding underneath me. As my husband and the nurse stood on either side of me, they each lifted a leg. The strange thing was my brain said my legs were still laying straight out in front of me. I could see the nurse and my husband lifting something heavy, but nothing was there! I could not see my legs! My brain wouldn't register them, because it still thought they were lying flat! Excuse the pun, but that was a real eye-opening experience for me. It made me realize we need a truth beyond what our eyes tell us.

It is the same with our other senses. We know that dogs can hear and smell things we can't. We can only see, smell, and hear a small amount of the total spectrum. We can only feel or touch things that have a frequency compatible to our own, like in the science video I just described with Dr. Moon. This is science. We can be living with another realm and be totally incapable of perceiving it! And, of course, that is exactly what the Bible has been telling us all along.

I hope your paradigm is being shook up like mine was when I first heard this stuff. We have been fed a lie. The lie is that science and the Bible are not compatible. It is that spiritual things are religious, but not scientific, that maybe God doesn't know as much as scientists! HA!

Wave Particle Duality

Let's look at another aspect of quantum physics. Studying these tiniest building blocks, subatomic particles called quanta, should be basic to understanding the nature of matter. What scientists found out studying these parts of atoms was astounding. Sometimes the electrons they were studying manifested themselves as particle of matter and sometimes they manifested merely as waves of energy. The difference being when they are being observed or measured, they act like what you would expect to find a tiny (extremely tiny) piece of matter, but when they are not being measured or observed they manifested as waves.

The experiment used (explained very basically) is the dual slit experiment. An electron is shot through a barrier with 2 slits toward a screen that records the patterns of how the electron then hits the back screen. The electrons did not appear to exist as matter at all, but were able to pass through both slits simultaneously and create wave patterns (similar to the interacting waves of two stones thrown into the water) on the screen recording the information at the back. When the scientists placed a measuring device into the experiment to measure the electron passing through the slit the result changed drastically. The electron then behaved as a particle. It only passed through one slit and made a dot on the rear screen. So, while being observed an electron is matter, but when it is not observed it dematerializes to a wave of energy.

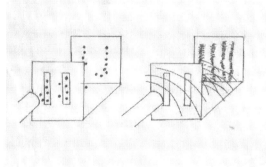

Dual Slit Experiment. While being observed photons acted like particles. While unobserved photons acted like waves of energy.

The implications of this are huge. If the building blocks of the universe could dematerialize in a moment, then couldn't the entire universe dematerialize in a moment!?

What holds it together?

What observer is watching the entire universe?

Does anything really exist?

Well our experience tells us we live in a stable universe. When I leave my empty bedroom and go into my kitchen, it doesn't disappear. How is it that we live in a material universe? What gives it its substance? Many scientists believe our universe is just a hologram or projection of a higher reality. What is that higher reality? Well, I believe the Bible gives us these answers.

Hebrew 11:1 says in the KJV "Faith *is the* **substance** *of things hoped for the evidence of things not seen*." I did a word study on this and the word for substance in Strong's Concordance is 5287 *hupostasis*. It means: giving substance or reality to, the essence, the substantial quality or nature of something. Literally the word is: **to stand under**. This verse is saying that faith is the substructure of things hoped for. It is the same word used in Heb 1:3 speaking of Jesus, *"And he is the radiance of His glory and the exact representation of His* **nature**...*"* The word nature is the same word as substance. Faith is the essence or true nature of things hoped for. Faith is the substance. Faith is what gives substance and holds the little waves of energy in place. Faith is the substructure of the universe. The word evidence is the number 1651 in Strong's Concordance. The Greek word is *elescho*: *to expose, bring to light*. Faith is what gives substance to and makes visible what it hoped for. Do you see it? The substance of the world is FAITH! Faith makes the difference. Faith takes waves of energy (*what is hoped for* is what the Bible calls it, the quantum physicist calls it *a possibility*) and makes it substance; it reveals it to this realm, so we can see it and experience it with our senses.

Regarding faith, Jesus said "*Truly I say to you, whoever says to this mountain, "Be taken up and cast into the sea, and does not doubt in his heart but believes that what he says is going to happen, it will be* **granted him** (these two words *granted him* are not in the original text, but added by the translators). The first part of that verse literally says, "...*does not doubt in his heart but believes that what he says will happen, it will be...*"

Faith causes what we say to *be*!

Unfortunately, this doesn't just work in the positive. It can also work in the negative. I heard a testimony once, where a woman had the thought, "You have cancer."

She thought it was God talking to her. She said aloud. "I have cancer." She, then went to the doctor and found out she had cancer. Because the whole thing seemed supernatural, she thought it was God. She didn't understand this principle. I believe this is science. Like if you drop a brick off a building, the law of gravity takes over. It is a scientific law. But then the verse goes on to talk specifically to believers. "*Therefore, I say to* **you**, *all things for which you* **pray** *and ask, believe you have received them, and they will be granted you*" Mark 11:23-24.

Jesus is saying, because that is true, when **you pray**, and ask use this principle. The word *pray* helps bring an understanding to the believer using faith as opposed to the unbeliever using faith. The Greek word for *pray* is *proseuxomai.* Bible Helps defines it this way: **Properly, to exchange wishes, pray-literally, to interact with the Lord by switching human wishes (ideas) for His wishes as He imparts faith (divine persuasion).**[3] When we as believers pray, we are in partnership with God. We are not begging God; we are together with Him bringing His will on the earth.

Do you see how at the beginning of this statement Jesus says "**whoever** says to this mountain 'Be taken up and cast into the sea and does not doubt in his heart but believes that what he says is going to happen, **it will be**"? He is giving a scientific principle, a blanket statement, that

---

[3] *Helps Word-Studies*, Helps Ministries Inc.,1987,2011https://biblehub.com/greek/4336.htm, accessed Oct.29,2019

could apply to anyone. Then He narrows down His statement, to the believer "**Therefore I say to you**" Because of the principle of faith, You believers when you pray, believe. Jesus is literally saying your faith will create your reality. If you believe, even something as inconceivable as a mountain moving into the sea will happen. Faith is what controls the material universe. (It is funny, now quantum philosophers and theorists are now saying these same things. They think it is new. Jesus, the one who created this whole thing gave us the inside scoop two thousand years ago!)

This "mountain" that Jesus is talking about, we think it is solid, unchangeable, immovable. The form and shape of the situations around us, they seem concrete. Jesus is saying it is a malleable substance. It is clay, changed and formed by the "hands" of faith. The universe seems to be shaped and formed by faith. It can be changed by faith! Jesus starts with a blanket statement, "whoever". It will work for anybody. It is a principle. It is a law of science, like gravity. But then He gets specific. Then He says to us, "therefore when **you** pray and ask". The Christian has the edge in this whole faith thing. We are connected to the "THE FAITH' the creative personal God. When we pray, we come into partnership and agreement with God and His will. Together we change the course of events. I don't think Jesus is talking about giving God your Christmas list. I think He is talking about coming into union with God and getting His will accomplished on earth. And that's why we have the edge. Our faith connected to God's will brings about a creative force.

Faith Speaks

2 Cor. 4:13 says *"But having the same spirit of faith, according to what is written, I believed therefore I spoke, we also believe therefore we also*

speak." Just like in the verse in Mark 11, this verse tells us faith is heart belief and then spoken words. Out the heart belief, words are spoken. That is faith. This is how God created the world.

We aren't like God, unfortunately, we say a lot of frivolous things we don't mean or shouldn't say. But God believes therefore: He speaks. He speaks from who He is. His words never come back void. How did God create? He spoke. He believed therefore He spoke.

If God has faith, what or who does He have faith in? Himself.

God revealed Himself to Moses as **I Am**. God is the only one who can say that. Everyone and everything else have their existence in the I Am. Our existence is totally dependent on God. Even the chair you are sitting on, it can't exist without God. God doesn't need us to exist.

He is.

Everything else needs Him. "For *in Him we live and move and exist*... "(Acts 17:28). When God swore to Abraham, He swore by Himself. There was no one greater to swear by. (Heb. 6:13). When He believes, He believes in Himself. What is the universe made of?

God's faith.

Where does that faith rest?

In God.

How was that faith released?

He spoke.

What did He speak?

Words.

Who is the Word?

Jesus.

And if there is a higher reality that we are merely a hologram of, what is the higher reality?

God.

God is the originator and sustainer of all matter and reality. All matter rests on the fact that God exists. So, God **is the only true reality.** God had to imagine us and all of creation. Then He got us in His heart and He believed. Then He spoke, and here we are. Everything is through Him and for Him and upheld by the word of His power. I like to say it this way "We are figments of God's imagination."

I was talking about this with my sister. She reminded me of a Guidepost magazine story we read years ago. A lady and her husband were spending the day together before a surgery that he was going to have the next day. They parked by the side of the road and found a lovely stream. They sat on a rock and enjoyed a wonderful, special time, feeling refreshed by the stream. When they got back to their car, as they were leaving, her husband realized he had left his pocket knife at the stream. She ran back to get it. The pocket knife was there beside the rock, but there was no stream! Only a dried-up stream bed. It didn't look like a stream had been there for years!

This might be difficult for many to believe. But in the quantum realm, reality is a set of possibilities, our material world is formed by faith. God has plenty of that! The woman in the story lost her husband the next day. In God's loving care, she had that beautiful last day. Who knows maybe the strange part of this story isn't that God formed a stream just for her, maybe the strange part is that she found out about it?

I remember seeing a testimony on the *It's Supernatural* television show. A car full of people were leaving an amazing revival meeting. As they were going through an intersection a vehicle to their left, a large camper, came barreling down a hill through the intersection unable to stop. As they cried out to the Lord, the vehicle passed right through them totally without causing any harm. This is crazy to our natural way of thinking. In God's realm, all he had to do was change their frequency to one that would not interact with the camper. Both of these miracles seem outrageous, almost unbelievable. Yet within the framework of the principles of quantum physics and the principles of faith, they are really almost scientific realities.

Time

Not only is matter different than what it appears to be, so is time. Picture, if you will, popping yourself out of this material world, out of all time, space and matter and inside of God, looking out of His eyes. There in front of you is the material universe and all time in one big unit. You see time is the fourth dimension. It is part of the material world. Scientists call the material universe the time-space continuum. It's one big unit. It started in his imagination and moved to His heart. He spoke it out of His mouth in faith. He created as a whole from the moment He said "Let there be light," until the events recorded in the book of Revelation chapter twenty-two when this temporal passes away and the eternal begins. He imagined and created it all. He sees the beginning. He sees the end. We are somewhere inside.

Chuck Missler explains the concept using this image.[4] Imagine sitting on the curb, watching a parade go by. As each float passes you, it appears to you as time is passing. But to someone up in a helicopter, the whole parade is happening all at the same time. The helicopter pilot is outside of the timeline of the parade. To him it is all one unit.

Picture yourself an author. You are writing a book. First you select the scene. You imagine it all, the towns, houses, gardens, and streets. You visualize it carefully so you can represent it realistically in your story. Then you imagine the characters one by one. You imagine their characteristics. You think about how they would react in each scene. You write the entire book. To the character inside the book life is happening scene by seen. To you, the book is a complete whole. (The difference between

[4] Chuck Missler, "A Message from Outside Time"
https://www.khouse.org/articles/2013/1123/print/, accessed Oct,25,2019

God's book and ours is each character has a free will!) God is outside the book. He can pick it up and read each page. But He knows how it begins and how it ends. Does God time travel? He doesn't need to! He is already there! He fills all time and space. I heard a wonderful minister, John Paul Jackson, say it this way: God is in your past right now. He is with you right now and He is already with you, right now, in your future. He is present in all time right now. (my paraphrase). I find that really comforting. God is with me in my future. He is already there, being Him, loving me, taking care of me!

The Scope of Creation

A piece of dust has approximately 3 million atoms, a drop of water 2 sextillion (that's a number with twenty-one zeroes!) Picture building the universe in quantum particles!   Yikes! we cannot even fathom that!

Max Planck, the father of quantum theory wrote, **"All matter originates and exists only by virtue of a force which brings the particle of an atom to vibration and holds this most minute solar system of the atom together. We must assume behind this force the existence of a conscious and intelligent mind. This mind is the matrix of all matter."**[5]

We know that creation involved the Father, the Son and the Holy Spirit. Genesis chapter one tells us that when God created, He spoke...when we speak, we speak a **word**.   John chapter one says "*In the beginning was the Word, and the Word was with God, and the Word was God. He was in the beginning with God. All things came into being through Him, and apart from Him nothing came into being that has come into being.*"   It seems to me from these scriptures that creation came from the mind and

[5] Max Planck Quotes, BrainyQuote.com ,Brainy Media Inc., 2019, https://www.brainyquote.com/quotes/max_planck_211839, accessed Sept 3,2019

heart of the Father. He spoke the Word who was Christ, the One who expresses the information and faith that gave substance to the material and spiritual world. The Holy Spirit hovered over creation, providing the power to shape it.

"*For by Him all things were created, both in the heavens and on earth, visible and invisible, whether thrones or dominions or rulers or authorities, all things have been created through Him and for Him. He is before all things and in Him all things hold together.*" (Col. 1:16-17) *Our* preincarnate Jesus is God and the matrix of all matter.

How big is Jesus? Bigger than the universe. How much information can He contain?   We already know omniscient means He knows everything, but that means enough to organize atoms of the entire universe together, and enough to know, in the most intimate sense, every human being that was ever created. He has a purpose and plan for their lives. Just like the infinitesimal sizes of quantum particles are difficult to grasp, and the astronomical sizes of outer space are impossible to grasp, we are not capable of grasping the mind or power of Jesus. But at the same time, He has taken that hugeness and confined it to finiteness, frailty, and the human condition, so that He could physically express His love and redemption to fallen man.   "*The Word became flesh and dwelt among us.*"

Here is an illustration of God's care, from my own experience with my husband.   I have always struggled with rejection and the ability to feel loved. In the earlier years of my marriage (before the Lord helped me), this carried over to my relationship with my husband, Walter. It was quite a trial to him. My husband and I have five children, although at the time this story took place, we only had four. We both felt it was important for me to be a stay at home mom, so we have lived, for the most part, off one income, while I stayed at home. One night I woke up and realized I was totally encased in my husband's love. I was sleeping in a bed he bought, in a room he had carpeted, trimmed, painted and decorated exactly the way I wanted. My house, my clothes, my dishes, even the food that I ate and became my physical body and kept me alive, my children, all lovingly provided to me by my husband and his hard work. Suddenly it all shouted love. I was totally surrounded by love, living in a world provided by his love. His love fed me, provided my needs, and built the "world" I live in.

What a picture of God. Sometimes He feels distant and aloof, but everything we have ever known, seen, heard, tasted, touched, smelled, experienced is a manifestation of His love, of His voice saying" *Let there be…*". We have never been outside or away from Him. Get the most powerful telescope. You won't be able to see outside of Him. The chair you sit on, the air you breathe, the sunlight, all matter, time and space held together by Him for you.

Remember the quantum particles only act like particles (or matter) if they are observed. Well, when you turn your back, does everything disappear? No, of course not. We live in a consistent material universe. So, what does that mean? God is there. He is all seeing, observing every atom from minute particles too small for us to fathom and huge distances of space too large for us to comprehend.

I hope the universe looks different to you now, like my home looked like a giant hug from my husband, I hope it looks like a giant hug from God. I hope when you look at the stars or a beautiful sunset, it shouts "God loves me. I am encased in His love." I hope the smell of a rose or a field of wildflowers says, "I am here with you. I love you. I won't leave you. I made this for **you**. Do you like it?"

"You have enclosed me behind and before and laid your hand upon me. Where can I go from Your Spirit, or where can I flee from your presence?" Psalm *139:* 5

Who is the pre-incarnate Jesus? Well, He is God. He is the Word. He is the quantum creator, the Faith person. Most of all, His power and mental capacity, His

27

love and compassion are way beyond our ability to fathom or comprehend.

Chapter 2

What Happened in the Garden of Eden?

In this chapter, I would like to go back to the beginning. I think an understanding of those first events in human history is important. It explains the reasons for why things are the way they are now. I know to some this narrative almost seems like a fairy tale. Some do not want to take it literally, but this is a big mistake. I grew up in the 60's and 70's. At that time, science and the Bible were considered incompatible. Anything spiritual was considered unscientific and naive.

I remember in my high school literature class, we were studying the Salem witch trials. It was all in the context of people and their motives. The teacher never even discussed the possibility of anything supernatural. There was a pastor's son in my class. He raised his hand and with much trepidation shared that he believed the spiritual realm was real and that he had dealt with some demonic things. I say he said it with trepidation, because at that time, it could have destroyed his reputation to say something like that. That was the mindset then. I think things have changed, but still many seem to be ignorant of the reality of the spirit realm, even in Christian circles.

What can sometimes appear to be poetic or symbolic in the Bible may be more literal than we realize. It is because the Bible is a book that deals with both realms. Things are different in that other realm. The Bible without explanation or apology states what happened from both a natural and spiritual perspective. So, with that in mind, let's look at what actually happened in the Garden of Eden. I believe that Adam and Eve lived in both the spirit realm and the physical realm simultaneously. I have four reasons for this.

Adam and Eve lived in the Physical and Spiritual Realm

First, Adam was created for fellowship with God, who is a Spirit (John 4:24), and Adam seemed to be able to walk and talk with Him freely. It would be odd for God to create a being to fellowship with, namely Adam, if he was incapable of seeing or hearing Him. I know we are in that position today, but that is because of the fall of man. I believe when God walked with Adam in the cool of the day, that they saw and conversed with each other.

Secondly, Adam and Eve seemed to be able to communicate with animals. When the serpent spoke to Eve, she didn't seem surprised that a creature was talking to her. She only responded to what he said. Many people who have had heavenly experiences talk about communication by thought. Heaven is filled with many kinds of creatures. All of them seem to praise God. I can't make a hard case for this, but it seems that if animals didn't communicate, a talking serpent would have thrown up some red flags.

Thirdly, Adam and Eve didn't know they were naked. I used to take that as 'they didn't know it was wrong to be naked', but it says they didn't **know** that they were naked. I believe they saw in the physical and the spiritual realms at the same time. They were clothed in the spirit with God's glory or light, and they didn't even see their nakedness. If we contrast Adam and Eve with the Church of Laodicea in the book of Revelation, Adam and Eve didn't know they were physically unclothed, while the church of Laodicea didn't know it was spiritually naked. Apparently, the church had much wealth in the natural realm, but had no knowledge of their spiritual condition.

"*Because you say 'I am rich, and have become wealthy and have need of nothing' and you do not know that you are poor and blind and naked, I advise you to buy from Me, gold refined by fire so that you may become rich, and white garments so that you may clothe yourself, and that the shame of your nakedness will not be revealed; and eye salve to anoint your eyes so that you may see.*" Revelation 3:17-18

The Church of Laodicea could only see in the physical. Their attention was focused on the outward man. They must have been very impressed with themselves, but they didn't know their true condition. They were blinded to the fact that in the spirit realm, they were shamefully naked. Adam and Eve saw both, but maybe the glory of their spiritual covering so outshone their physical nakedness, they didn't even notice their physical nakedness.

The fourth reason, I believe, Adam and Eve lived in both the physical and spiritual realms, is the world in the garden of Eden seems much like the heavenly world. What I mean by that is that there was a spiritual essence to physical things. We don't have trees of life around today that we can eat and live forever. We don't have food that gives spiritual benefit (except the Bible). The very thought seems almost like a fairy tale to us. And yet heavenly objects have a physical **and** spiritual essence.

In Revelation 5:8 "*When He had taken the book, the four living creatures and the twenty-four elders fell down before the Lamb, each one holding a harp and golden bowls full of incense, which are the prayers of the saints,*"

In the spirit realm or dimension, prayers have a substance and odor. We don't store our prayers in golden bowls. We can't smell them. We think of prayers more in the abstract. In the spirit, the essence and the substance are combined. Prayers are literally incense stored in bowls. Later in the book of Revelation, we also see bowls of God's wrath that are poured out on earth. Wrath is stored in bowls, and causes quite a stir when it is poured out! Here again we see something that for us is an attitude as being a substance. Wrath can be poured.

Roberts Liardon in the book We *Saw Heaven,* tells about the heavenly visitation he had when he was seven years old. This is what he says about praise.

"Praise is a substance. I saw all praise ascending out of the mouths of people as bright glowing vapors that collected at the top of the building. When the service was complete, the collected praise shot out of the top of the building and went to the throne room of God. I realized that praise and worship are not a routing or merely a preliminary to a message; they are a substance that is created."[6]

Roberts actually saw the praise of the saints while he was in heaven. Our praise and worship must also have a substance. We just can't see it in this realm.

How about spiritual clothing. I have a closet full of clothes. A have a lovely outfit brought back from India, when my niece went on a mission's trip. I have the dress I wore to my daughter's wedding. They are special. But none of them have a spiritual significance. They are just clothes. The Bible talks about robes of righteousness and a gown of salvation.

"For He has clothed me with garments of salvation, He has wrapped me with a robe of righteousness." (Is. 61:10)

But our own righteousness is a filthy rag.

"All of our righteous deeds are like a filthy garment." (Is. 64:6)

If we are depending on our own good deeds, in the spirit realm we are wearing dirty rags, but when we come

---

[6] Roberts Liardon, *We Saw Heaven*, (Shippensburg, PA 2000) pp,50-51

to Jesus, He clothes us with salvation. And it is actual clothing.

Jesse Duplantis talks about heavenly clothing in his book *Heaven Close Encounters of the God Kind.* Apparently when we are saved, we get a gown. But as we live for God, we add robes and other adornments to our clothing.

Brother Jesse says," **I was still dressed in my regular clothes, jeans and a shirt, but I noticed that many people coming from those vehicles were wearing beautiful, glorious robes. When they stepped out of the chariots, they ran straight toward the Holy City-they immediately took off for the Throne-shouting and praising God.**

Then I saw other people who didn't have on robes; they were wearing gowns. They started walking toward the city, but they seemed to get weak ...I asked the angel, "What's happening?'

He said, 'Some of them have not lived the life they should. They believe in God and love Jesus, but they didn't live to their fullest potential.'" [7]

As you can see from Brother Jesse's experience even our clothing represents our spiritual state. The strength of their body and ability to get to the Throne also was directly related to their spiritual condition. Here on earth, as I am sure you know, someone could win a bodybuilding contest and yet be spiritually bankrupt. The two do not correlate. They are not in the same dimension.

Seneca Sodi relates a similar situation in the book *Paradise, The Holy City and The Glory of the Throne*, **"In the distance I saw another chariot slackening its speed. Four souls clothed in the garments of heaven were seated within. To one of them I was particularly drawn. He was clothed in a white gown only. The moment he found he was**

---

[7] Jesse Duplantis, *Heaven Close Encounters of the God Kind*, (Tulsa, OK Harrison House, 1996) p.72

within the gates of paradise and opening his eyes upon the glory before him, he fell prostrate upon his face with deepest emotion, both of praise and regrets over the past. He was greatly bewildered over the glory of which he felt so unworthy. He tried to praise God but could not look up for shame, he was so nearly naked."[8]

The heavenly citizens are literally clothed in the nature of life they lived on earth.

This physical nature of things we think of as concepts in the spirit realm, is not only true of the beautiful side of that realm, but also of the evil side. The most life changing book I have personally read (beside the Bible) is *The Final Quest* by Rick Joyner. The whole book is a prophetic experience. In the book Rick describes how the army of Satan utilizes Christians. The scary fact is often they think they are doing the Lord's work, when in reality they are in Satan's army. These Christians were under the influence of different divisions of demons. They manifested the attributes of the demons they were under. It might be fear, pride, slander or a number of things. When they would hit other Christians with their arrows the wounded Christian would then respond in kind. If they received the arrow instead of using their shield of faith, they too would manifest the evil trait. I know I have done that. When someone speaks evil about me, my first response is to want to call everyone and talk about them. After reading this book, I realized more clearly what was happening. Rick describes this evil army. In the vision the army of Christians under the influence of demons was also overshadowed by vultures that made it difficult for them to see clearly. The vultures were vomiting condemnation on the captured Christians.

He writes," **Even worse than the vomit from the vultures** (that was condemnation) **was a repulsive slime**

[8] Rev. Elwood Scott, *Paradise the Holy City and the Glory of the Throne*, (Jasper, ARK, Engeltal Press) p.80

that these demons were urinating and defecating upon the Christians they rode. The slime was the pride, self-ambition etc. that was the nature of their division. However, this slime made the Christians feel so much better than the condemnation that they easily believed that the demons were messengers of God, and they actually thought this slime was the anointing of the Holy Spirit." [9]

Yikes! What a wakeup call!

Dr. Kynan Bridges shared a very similar vision on the *It's Supernatural* television show. In teaching about the dangers of slander, gossip, and offence, Dr. Bridges relays a vision he saw. Two women were talking outside after church. Each had a demon on her shoulder whispering lies. The women didn't even question these thoughts or take them captive. As they continued to talk, the demons vomited on them. The vomit was literally slander, gossip, and offence. They continued talking never realizing what was going on in the spirit realm. We know these things are sinful and wrong. But, rarely do we stop and think about the spiritual consequences of disobedience. I like to keep that picture in my mind in case I am tempted to gossip!

These things have a substance in the spirit. Just as the prayers and worship of the saints have a substance and a beautiful aroma, pride, slander, selfish ambition, and other sinful attitudes have a substance and aroma! I think we all have enough life experience to know how repulsive vomit, urine, and slime are! Yuck! Next time we are talking about someone in an unkind way, Lord, let us remember what is happening in the spirit realm!!!! I know many times I have had a sick feeling inside, like something just isn't right. If I get quiet and ask the Lord what it is, many times He has shown me that I have grieved Him with an unkind word or attitude against

---

[9] Rick Joyner, The Final Quest, (New Kensington, PA, Whitaker House, 1996) p. 21

someone. These things have a substance and odor! I think we can sense it. I have even felt that false sense of importance when I criticize others. Oh! now I know that it is demon slime!

In the garden, it seems that the two realms, spirit and physical, were somehow intrinsically intertwined. Even the shame of Adam and Eve's nakedness seemed to have a spiritual and physical nature about it. Fig leaves would make adequate clothing for physical nakedness. Animal skins require blood being shed which would cover sin and nakedness. Something happened in the garden, that separated the two worlds.

We know that we are spirit beings, that we live in a physical body and we have a soul. Yet, even though we are a spirit, we seem to be totally disconnected from the spirit realm. When Adam disobeyed God, what actually happened?

Gen.2:17 "but *of the tree of the knowledge of good and evil, you shall not eat, for in the day you eat from it you shall surely die.*"

Our translation says "surely die" but the Hebrew language actually says "in dying you will die".

I remember wondering why didn't Adam die when God clearly says "In the day you eat of it you will die". He did! That day his spirit died. An important thing to know is the Bible definition of death. Death is separation from God. Physical death is separation from our body. (Which can be good or bad depending on if you are spiritually alive or dead).

Adam died spiritually that day. Dying spiritually meant he was separated from God the source of life. Eventually nine hundred and some years later his body died.

Let's look at those same 4 points of how the world was both spiritual and physical after Adam died spiritually.

> 1. Adam could no longer walk and talk with God. He was separated from Him. Shame

and guilt caused him to hide from God. There was no more spiritual communion.

2. We can't talk to animals. The animal kingdom seems to operate on the principles of death. We have the 'food chain', not a love-based system. We know that when Jesus returns the lion will lay down with the lamb.
3. Adam saw that he was naked. He could no longer see into the spirit. He was not covered and clothed with God's glory.
4. Not only Adam, but all creation now seems to be separated from its essence.

Romans 8:20-22 says *"For the creation was subjected to futility not willingly, but because of Him who subjected it, in hope that the creation itself also will be set free from its slavery to corruption into the freedom of the glory of the children of God."*

In verse twenty *"creation was subjected to futility"* The word futility means: vanity, emptiness, unreality, purposelessness, ineffectiveness. One definition I found for vanity was lacking essence. Creation doesn't reflect the spirit realm. The two worlds were torn apart.

Four Dimensions or Ten?

Quantum physicists now believe that we live in 10 dimensions, but only 4 are knowable. That would be height, width, depth and time. I like to think of the four dimensions like this: what does it take for two points to meet? Let's say I wanted to meet a friend for coffee. We agree on an address. This gets me to two dimensions, length and width. But when I get to the address it is a twenty-five-story building! If I am on the first floor and she is on the tenth we will never meet. We have to be at the same height also. Let's say we get that right, too. We are both on the tenth floor. One more thing is necessary for us to meet. We have to be there at the same time. If I show up at ten and she comes at noon, we still won't meet. This is how I think of the four dimensions. What are the other six? We have no idea. They are probably as hard for us to conceive of as it is for a flat two-dimensional person to conceive of depth. You just couldn't explain it to them. The other six we seem to be separated from. I wonder, did Adam and Eve live in 10 dimensions? I sometimes wonder if those dimensions are things like love or faith. What is love? Is it a dimension? I don't know. The Bible says Jesus was moved with compassion. His compassion seemed to propel Him into a supernatural anointing where He would heal the sick. I don't know, but I like to wonder about these things.

Like I discussed earlier, the spirit world and the physical world may have been one whole, but now they are ripped apart by Adam's sin. Did the physical world once manifest spiritual realities? I think so.

How Satan Became the God of This World

In the garden of Eden, God gave authority of the earth to Adam. This authority is demonstrated in Adam naming the animals. Naming designates authority. We can only name what is ours, our children, our dog, our home, our car, etc. Names are also important to the identity of what is named. When Adam named the animals, God was transferring His authority to Adam. It would seem logical that God name the animals. He thought them up. He created them. He knew their specific functions and abilities. But He designated the earth to Adam. Adam named the animals.

In Gen. 1:28 we read, "*God blessed them and God said to them, 'Be fruitful and multiply, and fill the earth and subdue it, **rule** (have dominion, reign, rule) over the fish of the sea and over the birds of the sky and over every living thing that moves on the earth.*"

Adam was in a sense the god of this world, and God was the god of Adam. When Adam sinned, he exchanged gods. From Jehovah God, the I Am, the loving creator, to Satan, a tyrant and an enemy.

"Can the prey be taken from the mighty man, or the captives of a tyrant be rescued?" Surely, thus says the Lord, even the captives of the mighty man wall be taken away, and the prey of the tyrant will be rescued; For I will contend with the one who contends with you, And I will save your sons." Is.49:24-25

The human race and creation were separated from life, light and love and handed to a tyrant.

Spiritual Death and The Quantum Realm

Spiritual death is separation from God. Remember how we talked about the essence of creation being torn away, and the earth was subjected to futility. **God is the essence of creation.** If you don't mind stepping back into the quantum world with me. I see things more plainly there, and then I am able to switch back and understand the spiritual principles better.

Let's look at God, our quantum creator. Remember Max Planck's quote? **"All matter originates and exists only by virtue of a force which brings the particle of an atom to vibration and holds this most minute solar system of the atom together. We must assume behind this force the existence of a conscious and intelligent mind. This mind is the matrix of all matter."**[10] God is that intelligent mind and the matrix of all matter. He is good and all matter operates with beauty and order, because it operates according to His plan, His design, His order. The universe (time/space continuum) exists as He imagines, believes, organizes,

---

[10] Ibid.

39

speaks and holds it together. He is the source of all existence.

Everything else exists in Him. Then something happened. The creation rejected the creator. Pride gave birth to rebellion. The created being began thinking that it is somehow capable of being "I AM" instead of "in Him we live and move and have our being". In this aberration of the order and plan of God, chaos ensues.

There are two things in nature that I think illustrate the life of man (or fallen angel) in rebellion or not submitted to God. The first one is cancer. A normal cell has its instructions, the DNA (God's plan) of the cells. When it reproduces it follows the blueprint of the "I AM". It blesses and brings health to the whole body. A cancer cell does not follow the DNA. There is some sort of mutation. The cancer cell takes on its own identity. It uses the body's resources, but it does not follow the blueprint of the creator. It reproduces and becomes a foul cancerous mass, that feeds off the resources of the body and destroys it.

The Human Life without Christ

This is what we are like when in rebellion to God. We cannot produce love, goodness, life, or any good thing apart from submission to our Creator. I think we have lost touch today in our modern world with the definition of **God**. God means He is the boss. He is the highest authority. Actually, I think our culture has almost eradicated the understanding of authority. Everything is centered around the philosophy I *decide what is best for me, and as long as it doesn't "hurt" anybody, that is what is right.* There is no accountability, no understanding that we have to answer to someone for our choices and actions. There is no acknowledging that someone has the 'right' to tell me what to do.

My husband often quotes "*You shall know the truth and the truth will set you free.*" Then he explains wherever we are in deception, we are in bondage. Our society is in deception. Our society has cancer. It is unwilling to accept God's authority.

Another thing that demonstrates a life without God is a black hole. A star is supposed to shine out and give its light out. A black hole is when the star's gravitational pull becomes so great, it becomes a vacuum and instead of giving out light. It sucks all the light rays into itself. The human ego on the throne is like that black hole.

I remember when my kids were teens, a favorite saying they had was "I'm cutting you down, to build my self-esteem!" Self on the throne has to feed that ego. It is a vacuum. Like we used to say there is a God shaped hole inside of us. Our ego can never fill that God shaped hole. Even we, without God, are stripped of our essence.

In the 1970's when I got saved, there was a Christian tract that seemed to be everywhere. It was called *Have You Ever Heard of The Four Spiritual Laws?* In that tract was an illustration of a life with self on the throne and one with Christ on the throne. When Christ is on the throne everything is in order and peace.

When self is on the throne, everything is in chaos. Self on the throne is the original (Satan's sin) PRIDE.

Pride

I have my own definition of pride. Pride: an obsession with your own identity.
I use that definition because of my own journey. In the past I thought that pride was thinking that you are better than everyone else. Since I thought that I was inferior to everyone else, I figured I must be humble.

I spent much of my life trying to hide from attention. If my pencil lead needed sharpening in school, I wrote with a dull lead. Walking to the pencil sharpener was too intimidating. When I had conversations with people, I would rehash them in my head, trying to figure out if I had said the right thing. My sister made my phone calls, (although I made hers.) My sister even went on my first date with the boy who would later become my husband! (Ha ha, maybe that should have been a danger sign for him!)

What a revelation it was to me, as an adult, when a dear friend and prayer partner explained to me that pride has two manifestations. The way she put it, there are two sides to pride - PRESS: thinking your better than everyone, and CRUSH: thinking your worse than everyone. If the truth be told, even though I landed mostly on the "crush" side of pride, I did tend to swing the pendulum back and forth. I was obsessed with my own image: what people thought of me.

You might think it was kind of harsh to find out how prideful I really was, but it was SO FREEING!   Being afraid to do anything because of what people think of you is BONDAGE! Repenting of pride is freedom.

I remember an incident where this came very clear to me. It was at a ladies meeting for our church. We were planning an upcoming function of the group. I really like Holy Ghost freedom in meetings. I said something that I thought was the opinion of everyone there, about how the function should run. I really didn't think it was controversial at all, or I wouldn't have said it. But the room went quiet. That uncomfortable quiet, the kind that happens when there is a situation that no one knows how to handle. Then the Pastor who always seemed to be the one who smooths over touchy situations spoke up. He said some soothing words and the meeting went on. I wanted to get up and run out, but I sat there trying to look normal. I was hoping I could make it out the door before I started crying. I really thought the issue was these people didn't honor the Holy Spirit. I choked down the dessert (to look normal), and made a hasty exit.

As soon as I got in my car, I was sobbing. I didn't ever want to go back to the meeting or church for that matter. My heart literally felt like a knife was stabbing me.

I thought that I would be crying all night! I was driving and telling God how awful it was and that I could never go back. They did not want the move of the Holy Spirit and blah blah… About half way home the Lord spoke to me. He said "You think you are crying because they grieved the Holy Spirit, but you are really crying because they touched your pride." When He said those words all the pain was gone! I just said I was sorry for my pride, and I felt fine! I was shocked that I could feel so peaceful so quickly. The truth really does set you free.

The Whole Human Race Died in the Garden

Anyway, back to the garden. Adam disobeyed God and Satan became his god. God was in a sense an outsider in His own creation because of the authority and free will He gave to mankind. He is only Lord where mankind chooses to submit to Him.

When Jesus was in the wilderness being tempted by the devil, one of the temptations that Satan offered was to hand back to Jesus all the kingdoms of the world - if He would bow down and worship Him. Satan had gained legal access to the kingdoms of this world through Adam's sin. (Although God has always had people who chose Him.)

Luke 4:5 *"And he led Him up and showed Him all the kingdoms of the world in a moment of time. And the devil said to Him, "I will give You all this domain and its glory, for it has been handed over to me, and I give it to whomever I wish. Therefore, if You worship before me, it shall all be Yours."*

So, what happened in the garden? Adam died spiritually and as a result of that separation from God, physical death and corruption entered creation. Romans 8:7 says "because *the mind set on the flesh is hostile toward God, for it does not subject itself to the law of God, **for it is not even able to do so!** "*

We live in a body that is hostile to God. A body that is unable to be submitted to God! We can cry out with Paul in Romans 7:24 *"Oh wretched man that I am who will free me from the body of this death."*

The events that took place in the Garden of Eden changed the course of human history. Mankind fell into sin and the power of the enemy. The physical and spiritual realms were split apart. God, who is the essence of all creation, was no longer the center, order, and life of creation. Mankind was in need of a rescuer, a redeemer and a Savior. This is when the Second Law of Thermodynamics (that we talked about in chapter one) came into effect. The process of death began, not only in Adam, but in the universe. Everything began to move from order to chaos.

In the next chapter we will see how the world is able to continue on. It is because God's plan, His blueprint and design are still embedded in every living thing and is able to reproduce itself through the miracle of the seed.

Chapter 3
The Seed

Several years ago, I taught Creationism to three to five-year-olds. While teaching that class, I realized how much I didn't know. It really kept me on my toes and checking my facts. This was when I realized that God finished creation in 7 days. I had never really taken the time to ponder that His work was finished. He was all done.

Hebrews 4:4 ,10 *"For He has said somewhere concerning the seventh day 'And God rested on the seventh day from all His works...For the one who has entered His rest has himself rested from his works as God did from His."*

In my class our "experiment" was making marshmallow rice crispy treats, while we talked about the difference between something being created and made. We can only make things out of material that God created. We make things by putting things together, mixing or shaping, but we cannot create something from nothing. This is an impossibility for us. Because He is finished working, then something from nothing is an impossibility for our universe. (Unless He decides to make something.)

The Seed

As I prepared my lesson to explain this to little kids, I was struck with the importance of seed. The rice and sugar in our cookies certainly weren't created six thousand years ago. If it were not for that miracle of the seed, we would have run out of rice thousands of years ago. It became clear to me how miraculous and holy the seed is. The seed being untainted is what makes it God's creation. I looked in the dictionary for a definition of seed. It wasn't until I looked at the Webster's 1828 version that the definition seemed adequate. *"The substance, animal or vegetable which nature prepares for the reproduction and conservation of the species."* To me that barely scratches the surface. The seed seems to be an inanimate object, yet when properly planted contains the miracle of life and the information to reproduce the characteristics of its parents, perpetuating creation. The seed is a principle throughout scripture both in the natural and spiritual realm. Jesus used it to describe faith and the new birth. Science is a peek into God, his ways, and how He does things. The scientific principle of the seed gives us a peek into not only how things are reproduced in this natural world, but how they are reproduced in the spiritual realm. Remember in the last chapter we learned how the universe was once both physical and spiritual. It was a connected whole. Well then, the principles of reproduction in the spirit world and the natural world work on the same principles. Jesus talked about things like seeds, fields, and vineyards over and over, while He was explaining spiritual things.

Everything reproduces after its kind. Thoughts are seeds. Words are seeds. The gospel is a seed. The Bible is a seed. Jesus is a seed. Gifts given from the right motives are a seed. It is so simple, but so profound. An understanding of seed, makes Jesus teaching make so much more sense. Let's just be honest here, God is brilliant. He is a mastermind. How does He program the information and life to produce a plant or animal or person, into a little seed? Then that seed matures into a full-grown replica of its parents and produces more seed!

Ancient Seeds

In 1984, Chinese archeologists excavated an ancient tomb in the Fenghuang Mountains of China. The tomb was believed to be 2100 years old. Among other things they found ancient baskets. The archeologists covered the baskets with damp cloths for protection. To their surprise tiny seeds in the crevices of the baskets sprouted. The archeologists brought the sprouts to the Chengdu Agriculture Research Institute, who planted the sprouts. In seven months', time the seeds grew tomatoes. This caused quite a stir, because the accepted history of the tomato plant in China was that missionaries introduced them only 400 years before when they came into the country. Yet, 2100-year-old seeds found in a tomb produced tomatoes.[11] Two really good lessons here. One, seeds are amazing. Two, never accept the "accepted history".

When Were We Created?

Keeping in mind the principle of the seed, when did God create me? When did He create you? Before I understood what, I am about to explain, I actually had qualms about really believing that God created me. By that, I mean, that He created me in a personal sense. It seemed like He got the human race started. Then, it was pretty much a matter of random chance. If anyone really made the choice for my existence, it seems like it would have been my mother and father. I didn't feel like His personal creation. The key to when we were created, for me, was found in kind of a strange place: in Hebrews chapter seven in a discussion about the priesthood of Melchizedek.

Hebrews 7:9-10 *"And so to speak, through Abraham even Levi, who received tithes, paid tithes, for he was still in the loins of his father when Melchizedek met him."*

The argument presented is that the priesthood of Melchizedek is a higher priesthood than the Levitical priesthood, because Levi, while still in the loins of His

---

[11] Peng Ren, Tomato Find Sows Seeds of Doubt, *China Daily*, May 24, 1991, Chinadaily.com.cn, accessed Jan.6.2019

father Abraham, paid tithes to Melchizedek. This act designating that Melchizedek was the superior of the two priesthoods. An interesting study and an interesting argument. I would never have dared make this argument. I find it intriguing. Obviously, Paul or the Holy Spirit who wrote this had some insight I could never have imagined. So, in the eyes of scripture, which I would equate with God's opinion, Levi paid tithes hundreds of years before he was born. Levi was present in Abraham's loins, specifically his DNA was present, therefore he existed. Crazy huh? Hundreds of years before he was born, in God's eyes he existed. So back to my question, when did God created me and you?

He created us on the sixth day of creation. The day He created Adam.

He didn't just create one man. He created the whole human race. He planned every single human being. Somehow allowing for free will, He could see every person and planned their heritage, characteristics, personalities, giftings, and planned a perfect will and destiny for each person. He also had a route to salvation. He had a plan to redeem our mistakes and failures when they are brought to Him. It was all there on day six. He **did** personally create you and me, it was in the miracle of the seed. Our DNA was carried in Adam.

We know from Psalm 139:16 *"Your eyes have seen my unformed substance and in your book were all written the days that were ordained for me when as yet there was not one of them."*

When was that book written? Not a day, week or month before we were born, (like I used to think). It was written when God created Adam (if not before). There are some very interesting words in this passage. *"Your eyes have seen my unformed substance."* The word for *substance* in Hebrew is *galemi*. It is the noun form of the verb *"to wrap"*. One entry I found on biblehub.com translated this word: *a wrapped substance*. I think of the spiral of the DNA. Could this word be a reference to DNA? *"Your eyes have seen my wrappings, or wrapped substance."* Physically as far as this material realm goes, we were DNA when God created Adam. DNA is information. The information needed to decide what you are. It was inside of Adam. Just as Levi was inside of Abraham.

"And in your book, they were all written" I have wondered if that book could possibly be our DNA. In a video called *The Atheist Delusion*,[12] Ray Comfort presents a book to a group of self-proclaimed atheists. He asks each one if the book could just create itself. Of course, each says no. Then he presents to each atheist the amazing facts of our DNA. It is in every cell of our body and called the instruction book of life. It is a complex language that contains 3.2 billion letters. As Ray Comfort explains "**if you stretched your DNA end to end, it could go to the sun and back three times**." This is an incredibly complex book written in every cell of your body. This video can be watched in its entirety on the website www.theatheistmovie.com.

When God created Adam (and Eve who came out of Adam) he encoded not only Adam and Eve and foreknew each of their children, but every human being ever to be born. He foreknew, fore planned, and wrote the book as he created Adam. You were, in a sense already, created when God created Adam.

The Human Spirit

Now we know that human beings are not just a physical body, there is the God breathed spirit in every human being. We are not just physical bodies. We are spirit beings that have a soul and live in that body that Adam carried. At conception, as that first spark of life takes place, our spirit enters our body. Jesse Duplantis, Kat Kerr and Neville Johnson have all had visitations to

[12] Ray Comfort, "The Atheist Delusion" wwwatheistmovie.com/about

the Throne Room of God. They all describe seeing little spirits coming out of the Father.

Jesse Duplantis relates his experience in the book *Heaven Close Encounters of The God Kind* "**I saw new lives of little babies singing and flying around God's Throne. It seemed to me that babies just came out of the breath of God. They looked like they were wearing nightgowns. They flew into the presence of Jehovah. I realized they were new souls who came from the thoughts of God. God thinks kids. Now I know why those newborn babies are so precious. Babies are gifts given to us directly from the Throne of God. I heard them say to God, "Can I be a spirit? Would You send me to earth so I can be a spirit?" And while I watched, I heard the mighty sound of God's power. Whoosh! I saw these babies leave the Throne by the power of God.**"[13]

We are beings created in God's imagination! The information, the seed of our physical body, or of the human race was carried in Adam. The spirit was carried in the mind or heart of God!

This miracle of the seed is expressed in the creation narrative and throughout scripture. Genesis 1:12 "*The earth brought forth vegetation, plants yielding seed after their kind…*" Like I explained to my preschool class, God created trees and flowers and every kind of plant, but without the seed, when that tree died it would have become extinct. It is in the miracle of that holy seed we still have each kind of tree. It is created by God.

So, to review, we were all created on the sixth day. Our physical being was inside of Adam. Our spirit was in the mind and heart of the Father in heaven. Just as Levi was in Abraham we were in Adam. We see that seed is holy. It is the blueprint and physicality of creation. It produces after God's plan, after its own kind.

---

[13] Jesse Duplantis, *Heaven Close Encounters of the God Kind*, (Tulsa, OK, Harrison House, 1996) p. 119

Chapter 4

The Attack on The Seed

When God created the world, it was good. He was the center of creation. All creation was submitted to Him and gave glory to Him. Creation was life, love, and glory filled. God IS the essence of everything. This is how heaven is. This is the proper order of things. If man or Satan is the center, and all is for his glory, then this brings destruction and death. We are NOT the I AM. We are not capable of emanating life and love and order apart from God. We become a vacuum, not an outshining.

If Adam and mankind would have submitted to God, there would have been no death, disease, abuse, selfishness, etc. The earth would have remained a paradise. It would have been ruled by the love of God.

Adam sinned in the Garden of Eden by eating of the Tree of the Knowledge of Good and Evil. Adam caused the death of the human race who he carried within himself. When God confronted the serpent, Adam, and Eve, about their disobedience, He cursed the serpent. Then He gives the first reference to a redeemer, Christ the Man. By *"Christ the Man"* I am not referring to Jesus the eternal Word who has always existed with the Father, even though He is the same person. I am talking about the plan of God, the legality of the eternal God coming in human form as our Savior and Redeemer. So here we have the first reference or prophecy of Jesus the Man in

Gen. 3:15. *"I will put enmity between you (the serpent) and the woman. And between your seed and her seed. He shall bruise you on the head. And you shall bruise Him on the heel".*

We, the entire race of fallen human beings, are the seed carried in Adam. But Jesus the man is **THE SEED** of the woman. In the conception of a child, man carries the seed therefore, we already see a foreshadowing of the virgin birth. We also can see that Jesus the Man is not **in** Adam. He does not inherit spiritual death with the rest of us. Here begins the epic story of our heroic rescue.

The entire Bible, I believe, is the story of our Redemption. It is the story of Christ Jesus the Man. Each book records the journey of The Seed from a promise to a legal reality. We see Him carried by a man with a covenant, by a family, by nation, by a dynasty of kings, by a virgin. We see Him planted in the earth. We see Him bursting forth from the ground in resurrection, bearing much fruit. We see Him multiplied in the earth in His own people. We see Him returning as Bridegroom to the church and King to Israel. We see Him summing up all things in heaven and earth to an administration suitable to the fullness of the times! This is the epic that is our Bible. This is the story of our Christ Jesus the Man.

Running along this beautiful narrative of redemption, we see the war on the seed. This war is on the blueprint of God for each part of His creation, and the war is on The Seed, our redemption, Christ the Man. Like we talked about earlier, the seed is God's will and plan for creation. It also carries that divine life to reproduce the life of the parent. If you were to cut down a tree, you have only destroyed that one tree. It can be reproduced over and over again. But if you destroy the seed, you have destroyed every tree.

Throughout the course of history, this has been Satan's objective. If he can destroy the seed, he can destroy the fingerprint of God on creation. The principle of seed is throughout creation both in the physical and spiritual realm. The crowning seed of all mankind, was Christ. He was the main objective. But every seed is important. Whether it is human, animal, plant, truth, the Word of God, etc.

The Seed Carries God's Plan

James 1:17-18 says *"Every good thing given and every perfect gift is from above, coming down from the Father of lights, with whom there is no **variation** or **shifting shadow**. In the exercise of His will He brought us forth by the word of truth, so that we would be a kind of first fruits among His creatures."*

The words for both *variation* and *shifting* are two different words, but both can refer to mutation. What God created was perfect. He placed within it the ability to reproduce perfectly, to represent His intention without change or mutation. I am going to quote the definition for shadow from the website biblehub.com Helps Word-Studies because it is so appropriate to what we are talking about. (The numbers refer to the Strong's concordance numbers for each word.)

"644 *aposkiasma* (from 575 *apo* 'from' and *skiazo* 'cast shade') properly a *shadow* created by turning. Typically, shadows change according to the changing position of the sun (being short at midday and lengthy at nightfall) But *God doesn't change (shorten or lengthen)* because He Himself is the only absolute reference point! Unlike a *shifting* shadow caused by revolution. The Lord is immutable and possesses all power and life *in Himself.*"[14]

God is the reference point for all truth- **all** truth, that includes genetic truth. He is the reference, the truth of all creation. This means your eye color, the stars and planets, your talents and abilities, the plan He has for your

---

[14] *Helps Word-Studies*, Helps Ministries Inc., 1987, 2011, https://biblehub.com/greek/644.htm, accessed Feb 21,2019

life, or even the plants in your yard. What an apple is supposed to look and taste like. Everything.

We saw in the last chapter, from the very beginning death entered the DNA of mankind. Even before a single child was born, the curse of death entered the seed. Let's look at other attacks on the seed.

Genesis chapter 6 is only three chapters away from the Garden of Eden, but it is about 1500 years later. I think it is hard for us to relate to approximately 900-year life spans. If we had those kinds of lifespans it would mean we would have born back in the Robin Hood times! It is crazy to think about. Modern indoctrination causes us to think these early people were primitive, but this just isn't so. Forbidden archaeology and OOPARTS (an acronym for out of place artifacts), have been swept under the sociologist's rug. These people were not cavemen. Recent studies by Tom Horn, L.A. Marzulli, Steve Quayle, Timothy Alberino and others show that these ancient people had technology we haven't been able to explain or duplicate today. The most famous being the pyramids, but all over the world there are massive preflood remains of structures built with massive stones we couldn't move today with all of our technology. Now the history channels and science television shows are finally talking about some of these things, but using the narrative that aliens came to earth. This is a distortion of the truth. The" aliens" they are talking about were in the Bible all along, as we will soon see. I would highly recommend anyone interested googling the names of the Christian researchers I listed above and getting some of their fascinating material to study (or watch).

Noah

Gen. 6:1-4 ,12 *"Now it came about when men began to multiply on the face of the land, and daughters were born to them, that the sons of God saw that the daughters of men were beautiful; and they took wives for themselves, whomever they chose. Then the Lord said, "My Spirit will not strive with man forever, because he also is flesh; nevertheless, his days shall be one hundred and twenty years.' The Nephilim were on the earth in those days, and also afterward, when the sons of God came in to the daughters of men, and they bore to them. Those were the mighty men of old, men of renown…. God looked on the earth, and behold, it was corrupt; for all flesh had corrupted their way upon the earth."*

Fallen angelic beings interbred with women and were corrupting the seed of mankind. The animals were also being corrupted. The word for *corrupt* in verse 12 *"all flesh had **corrupted** their way upon the earth."* is translated destroyed in most verses. God's blueprint for humanity was being destroyed through corrupt sexual practices. The Berean Study Bible translates this verse: *"And God looked upon the earth and saw that it was corrupt, for all living creatures on the earth had corrupted their ways."*

Jude 1:6-7 says *"And angels who did not keep their own domain, but abandoned their proper abode, He has kept in eternal bonds under darkness for the judgement of the great day, Just as Sodom and Gomorrah and the cities around them, since they in the same way as these indulged in gross immorality and went after strange flesh, are exhibited as an example in undergoing the punishment of eternal fire."*

The flood of Noah wasn't just a judgment. It was preservation! The seed of man and animals was being destroyed. Satan's attack on the seed was in full force. Mankind was corrupted, destroyed, no longer pure. Mankind's DNA blueprint was no longer strictly human. The fallen even interbred with animals and corrupted their DNA. Satan was trying to prevent Christ the Man, the seed of woman, from coming. His plan was tainting the seed!

The Jewish historian Josephus writes of this **" For many angels of God coupled with women, and begat** sons that proved unjust and despisers of all that was good, on account of the confidence they had in their own strength; for the tradition is, that these men did what resembled the acts of those whom the Greeks call giants (Titans)."[15]

God cleansed the earth with the flood. He replenished the earth with only Noah's descendants. Gen. 6:9 says (KJV) *"These are the generations of Noah. Noah was a just man and perfect in his generations and Noah walked with God."* The phrase *"perfect in his generations"* seems odd. The word perfect is actually the same word *unblemished,* used in Exodus 12:5 referring to the Passover lamb: *"Your lamb shall be an **unblemished** male".*

I believe this odd phrase is saying that Noah's seed was uncontaminated. It was not profaned with the seed of fallen angels.

The book of Enoch, although not scripture, was important to the Jewish culture and quoted in the Bible. It says in Enoch 10:1-3 **"Then the Most High, the Great and Holy One, said to Uriel,' Go to the son of Lamech (Noah) and tell him in my name, 'Hide thyself' Reveal to him the judgement that is approaching: that all life will be destroyed by a flood of water that will cover the entire earth. Instruct him how he may escape and his seed may be preserved throughout all the generations of the world."**[16]

God was preserving the seed. The purpose of the flood was to preserve the seed. Without that seed humanity wouldn't be what God created it to be, and the redeemer could not come. The flood wasn't about destruction as much as it was about preservation.

---

[15] Josephus, Jewish Antiquities, 1,3,1(73), *The Complete Works of Josephus*, Translated into English by William Whiston, (Kregel Publications, Grand Rapids Mi.1999) p.53

[16] Ken Johnson, Th.D., *Ancient Book of Enoch*, (2012) p.21

Balaam

Another attack we see against the seed is the story of Balaam, the man most known for his talking donkey. After the children of Israel came out of Egypt, and were in the wilderness, they destroyed some of the cities of the Amorites and Og, the King of Bashan. These were the first of the evil inhabitants of the promised land to be destroyed. A nearby king, Balak, the king of the Moabites, became alarmed that he would be next. He called on Balaam, a Midianite prophet of God. Balak, the pagan king, asked Balaam, the prophet, to curse the children of Israel. Balak was afraid of Israel, and knew whomever Balaam cursed was cursed.

Balaam comes, but instead of cursing God's people, he blesses them three times. Balak is angry and tells Balaam to go home. Balaam prophesied once more and then leaves. Apparently before he left, he gives Israel's enemies a strategy for destroying them. In the next chapter we see Israel playing the harlot with the daughters of Moab, and they also joined themselves to the false god, Baal of Peor. Here again is an attack against the seed. This time the attack is specifically against the nation of Israel, who now carries the seed of The Man, Jesus. Israel is to be a holy people set apart to God. They are not to intermarry or join in worship of false gods. Balaam with all his flowery speeches about how he follows and obeys God, shows his true motives. He teaches the Midianites to seduce the men of Israel to commit immoral acts and worship false gods. He does this through the beautiful daughters of Midian. This was a corruption of the seed of Israel. I do not know if there was Nephilim blood specifically in the Midianites. We do know there were giants in the promised land. This could have been another infiltration of demonic seed or an infiltration of the *other* demonic seed: rebellion and idolatry. In either case it was an attack against the seed. We see quick and harsh retribution. Numbers 31:16 says *"Behold these*

(Midianite women) *caused the sons of Israel, through the counsel of Balaam, to trespass against the Lord in the matter of Peor so the plague was among the congregation of the Lord."* A plague killed 24,000 Israelites, until it was stopped by Phineas the priest. Phineas in his zeal for the Lord killed Zimri, who in the sight of everyone had brought Cosbi, a prominent Midianite woman into his tent. (It is interesting to note the name Cosbi means deception. Zimri brought deception into the camp!) Now the attack on the seed, could be narrowed down to the nation of Israel. They were to be a holy nation, set apart to God. They were set apart to carry the Seed, Jesus the man.

The Parable of The Sower

In the New Testament, the kingdom of God becomes a spiritual kingdom, born of spiritual seed-the Word of God. Although, I want to come back to this portion of scripture later in the book, I'd like to take a look at it now, through the lens of "the attack on the seed." The scripture I am talking about is the Parable of the Sower. This parable describes the attack against the Word of God, to keep it from bearing fruit in the human heart. Matt 13:3-9,18-23 *"Behold the sower went out to sow; and as he sowed, some seeds fell beside the road, and the birds came and ate them up. Others fell on the rocky places, where they did not have much soil, and immediately they sprang up, because they had no depth of soil. But when the sun had risen, they were scorched; and because they had no root they withered away. Others fell among the thorns, and the thorns came up and choked them out. And others fell on the good soil and yielded a crop, some a hundredfold, some sixty, and some thirty. He who has ears, let him hear…. Hear then the parable of the sower. When anyone hears the word of the kingdom and does not understand it, the evil one comes and snatches away what has been sown in his heart. This is the one on* *whom seed was sown beside the road. The one on whom seed was sown on the rocky places, this is the man who hears the word and immediately receives it with joy; yet he has no firm root in himself, but is only temporary, and when affliction or persecution arises **because of the word**, immediately he falls sway. And the one on whom see was sown among the thorns, this is the man who hears the word, and the worry of the world and the deceitfulness of wealth choke the word, and it becomes unfruitful. And the one on whom seed was sown on the good soil, this is the man who hears the word and understands it; who indeed bears fruit and brings forth, some a hundredfold, some sixty, and some thirty."* Jesus tells the parable and then gives the interpretation to his disciples. The seed is the word of the kingdom. Here we can see a list of attacks that come against the Word.

1. Don't understand it
2. The evil one snatches it away
3. Lack of root or depth
4. Affliction
5. Persecution
6. Worry of the world
7. Deceitfulness of riches

These are attacks that keep the Word from producing in our lives. The Word carries God's plan, God's spiritual seed or DNA that produces His plan in our lives. Notice one verse says affliction and persecution arise **for the word's sake,** meaning, specifically coming to remove the word. Did you ever notice when you try to move out in an area, immediately things seem worse? There is a reason for that. It is designed to get the word out of your heart, to get you to say, "well, I guess that doesn't work."   It is an attack against the seed.

After this parable, Jesus gives a warning, perhaps even specifically for the people of our generation, although Satan has been using the same tactics throughout the ages. Mark 4: 24-25 *"And He was saying, to them "Take care what you listen to, by your standard of* measure it will be measured to you: and more will be given to you besides." Luke says it this way…" *Take care* **how** *you listen…."* He is giving a warning, what about? TRUTH. That's what is under attack here TRUTH. That is what the seed contains. God's word, God's plan is truth. The word Jesus uses for "take care" is the Greek word "*blepo*" it can mean: *earnestly contemplate, properly to see, be observant*. The warning is: earnestly heed truth. If you do, you will get more. But if you don't, you will lose what you have!

The Amplified Bible says it this way, "*And He said to them, 'Be careful what you are hearing. The measure [of thought and study] you give [to the truth you hear] will be the measure [of virtue and knowledge] that comes back to you, and more [besides] will be given to you who hear."*

Truth is dangerous to the enemy. Truth is being targeted, muddied, and confused. I think that this battle is getting more and more obvious. We hear everyone screaming "Fake News." It is getting to be a joke and a catch phrase. Everyone's idea of which news is the true news and which is the fake news is different! Romans chapter one talks about the decline of truth as men's hearts grow evil. My husband has a wonderful teaching about the connection between our ability to receive and perceive truth and the condition of our hearts. The purer our heart, the better able we are to see clearly. As the 'be attitude" states "*Blessed are the pure in heart, for they shall see God."* Romans 1:21-22,25 tells us the opposite side of that spectrum. "*For even though they knew God, they did not honor Him as God or give thanks, but they became futile in their speculations, and their foolish heart was darkened. Professing to be wise, they became fools…They exchanged the truth* **of God for a lie...**"

Let's take a moment to think about what is truth and what is a lie. Not only is truth under attack, but the very concept that there is such a thing as truth is under attack.

When we as humans refuse to accept that the standard of truth has to come from outside of ourselves, then all truth becomes subjective. There is no longer a standard of truth, but only what seems right to me and what seems right to you. We have to have a standard outside of ourselves.

I remember quite a few years back; I painted a winter village scene on a tin plate. Something about it looked off to me, but I didn't know what. I showed it to my husband who is a carpenter. He immediately pointed out what was wrong. I had painted the houses on the angle of the hills. My husband explained to me, if you build a home on a hill, it still has to be level. It can't follow the angle of the hill.

Carpenters use a plumb line or a level when they build. A plumb line is simply a string covered with chalk that is hung from a nail. It has a weight at the end. Gravity pulls it level or perpendicular to the ground and your snap the string against the wall and it leaves a line that is plumb or straight. If you didn't do this, your house would be crooked and weak.

Mystery Spot

I live in Michigan in the lower peninsula. If you cross the Mackinac Bridge that connects the upper and lower peninsulas of Michigan, just north of the bridge is a tourist site called Mystery Spot. I remember my family went on a vacation to the upper peninsula when I was a little girl. My sister and I saw cars everywhere that had bumper stickers that said "I went to Mystery Spot". I had no idea what it was, but my curiosity was piqued! We pestered our parents until they took us to Mystery Spot!

Mystery Spot was simply a shack built into a hill, so that the whole house was angled and tipsy turvy. The floor and walls were so slanted that is no longer possible to tell what was and what wasn't level. What made it so fun was that the angles of the structure created so many optical illusions: tall people looked shorter than short people, balls and water seem to travel uphill, and chairs seemed to balance on nothing up against a wall. When the "truth" of what is level is gone, one loses the ability to perceive what is normal, simple, and obvious, (like what is uphill, downhill or level). This is how truth works. We have to have a standard outside of ourselves and our own perceptions.

What is Truth

So, we need to answer the question "What is truth?" I think it is interesting to note in the Hebrew the word for *truth* is also *firmness or reliability*, In Greek, the word truth can also mean *reality*. We could say that truth is that which makes something firm, reliable or real. Let's go back to that quote from Max Planck, the father of quantum physics. **"All matter originates and exists only by virtue of a force which brings the particle of an atom to vibration and holds this most minute solar system of the atom together. We must assume behind this force the existence of a conscious and intelligent mind. This mind is the matrix of all matter."[17]**

The matrix of all matter is God. He is the source and sustainer of all matter-so He has to be the source of reality and truth. Jesus confirms this when He says "*I am the way, the truth and the life.*"

That is not wording we really understand. Jesus didn't say, 'I know the truth, I tell the truth or I act truthfully." He said "*I AM the truth.*" God, Himself, is truth and reality.

Romans 1:18,19,21,25 talks about truth and also the lie.

*"For the wrath of God is revealed from heaven against all unrighteousness of men who **suppress the truth in unrighteousness**, because that which is known about*

---

[17] Ibid.

*God is evident within them; for God made it evident to them… For even though they knew God, **they did not honor Him as God** or give thanks, but they became **futile** in their speculations and their foolish heart was darkened… for they exchanged **the truth of God for a lie** (literally it says THE lie) and **worshipped and served the creature rather than the Creator**, who is blessed forever.'*

God is truth. When we move toward God, we move toward truth. What I mean by *moving toward God*, is honoring Him as God, submitting our will to Him in obedience. This is truth because He is God. He created you. Therefore, He knows your purpose. He knows your value. That is the truth about you. You didn't think yourself up. He did. His plan is your truth. What He says about you is your truth. Not anyone else, including yourself, can decide your purpose and value. All created things should be submitted to Him as God. This is the correct order.

I think we have all been at a grocery store or some other public place and seen a child throwing a fit and disrespecting his parents. What is even worse is when we see the parents cowing down to the child and letting them be in charge. This is repulsive and uncomfortable, because it is dishonoring and disrespectful. It is not the proper order of the family. The child is not capable of being in charge. The parents are.

How much more is God the proper authority of every part and person of creation. To not honor Him is repulsive and out of order. As a matter of fact, if we look carefully at verse 25, I think we can see this is not just *A lie*, but it is *THE lie*. I am going to paraphrase this verse a bit. *"They exchange the truth and reality of God for **the** lie, and worship and served their own selves, a created being, rather than the Creator who only good can be said of Him forever."*

The lie is that we can exist apart from God. That we are autonomous. When we are in rebellion to God, we are acting out a lie. And moving so far from the truth, it is like we are morally in a Mystery Spot. We can no longer see the world in true perspective.

What is THE Lie?

Jesus called Satan a liar and the father of lies. *"You are of your father the devil, and you want to do the desires of your father. He was a murderer from the beginning, and does not stand in the truth because there is no truth in him. Whenever he speaks a lie, he speaks from his own nature, for he is a liar and the father of lies."* (John 8:44)

Lying originated from Satan. Let's look and see where the first lie originated. This is in the prophetic account of the fall of Satan in Isaiah 14:13-14 *"But you said in your heart, I will ascend to heaven; I will raise my throne above the stars of God, And I will sit on the mount of assembly in the recesses of the north. I will ascend above the heights of the clouds;* **I will make myself like the Most High."** This is *THE lie. That we can be like God.* **The lie** is the root out of which every other lie grows. When we try to be like God, we are deceived and must lie and deceive to feed the vacuum that self-worship and pride becomes. Satan not only took on this lying nature, he spread it to mankind, by deceiving Eve. Genesis 3:4-5 *"The serpent said to the woman, 'You surely shall not die! For God knows in the day that you eat it, your eyes will be opened and* **you will be like God** *knowing good and evil."* This was total deception. Yes, they did die. God was not withholding from man; Satan was just causing Eve to doubt God's love and kindness. He was tempting her to be her own God. Even this was a lie, because rebellion to God is slavery to sin and Satan. These are hard masters.

Did God Create Evil?

I have heard the question if God is good, why would He create evil? I think a clearer understanding of science will help clear up this misconception. We tend to think of darkness as the counterpart to light and cold as the counterpart to heat. We think of these as two opposing forces with opposite characteristics. But this is not true. Darkness is simply the absence of light. Cold is the absence of heat. Light and Heat are energy. They **are** something. Darkness and cold are not 'a thing'. They are what happens when the 'thing' is gone!

If you can broaden that to life and death, good and evil, truth and deception, love and pride, you can get a glimpse of something bigger!

Light, energy, life, truth, goodness, love these are ALL God!!!! If you remove God from creation, what do you get? Darkness, entropy, death, deception, evil, and pride. God didn't create the removal of Himself! He is All and fills All, but if you reject Him, the result is the lack of Him. So, Satan and man create evil. Evil is creation minus God. Evil is what happens when the creation rejects the creator. Evil is the result of the created thing seeking its own identity or its own glory rather than realize that God is the identity of creation. To obey and glorify Him is the fulfillment of our identity.

Wow! It took me a really long time to understand this truth. My whole life feels like it has been a struggle to find my identity. The answer all along was to lose it!

Thanks, I Needed That

This makes me think of the verse in the book of James 3:16, "*For where jealousy and selfish ambition exist, there is disorder and every evil thing.*"

My twin sister and I were the television generation.

The generation today is the internet generation. If my kids or grandkids say something that makes no sense to me, I know they are quoting a 'meme'. For my sister and I, however, television and old movies formed a lot of our understanding of the world. It seemed like in many of the shows and movies when a character got out of touch with reality, their best friend would slap them across the face. They would always respond with "Thanks, I needed that!" I can picture Bob Hope saying this to Bing Crosby, but I have seen this in many shows. In fact, I thought that was the right thing to do! One time when my sister was freaking out about something, I slapped her across the face. I totally expected her to say, 'Thanks I needed that!' I was shocked when she was furious and came after me!

Well, I have learned that, that only works in the movies, but this verse in James, *"For where jealousy and selfish ambition exist, there is disorder and every evil thing."*, this is my slap in the face Bible verse. I think about it when the ugly, selfish nature wants to rise up. It slaps me in the face, and I say "Thanks, I needed that."

I have talked about "truth" in the heart issues. But the genetics, the DNA of every created thing is God's "truth" for that thing. God created everything to reproduce after its kind. If we tamper with the DNA; we have changed God's truth. This is just another progression in the development of THE lie. The attack of the seed is Satan's method of removing God from His creation.

Genetic Manipulation

If you have a garden or even if you are just a nutrition conscious grocery shopper, you have probably already become aware of the "attack of the seed" on our food supply. It began with hybrid seeds. These seeds don't seem to be too diabolical. They won't kill you if you eat them. They just don't reproduce after their own kind. We know from the Bible; seed is supposed to reproduce after its own kind. Not too big of an inconvenience in our gardens. Most of us don't save our own seed anyway. But on a global scale, particularly in third world nations the results were devastating. Many small farmers were promised greater yields and uniform produce. What they ended up with were seeds that needed more fertilizer and water. Even more devastating these seeds did not reproduce after their kind. Most third world farmers were not able to afford these new costs. They lost their homes and livelihoods. Dawn Gifford from the website smallfootprintfamily.com explains, "**This is how the massive, infamous slums of India, Latin America, and other developing countries were created ...And once these farmers sold or abandoned their land, guess who bought it all up? That's right Agribusiness. Hybrid seeds were the seminal foundation of corporate-controlled industrial petrochemical-dependent monocultures.... The world lost an estimated 75 percent of its food biodiversity, and control over seeds shifted from farming communities to a handful of multinational corporations**"[18]

Apparently controlling the seeds of the world isn't enough. Enter GMO seeds! These seeds literally have their DNA tampered with. The book *Seeds of Deception* by Jeffrey Smith documents the battle of GMO seeds in Europe. One particular scientist Arpad Pusztai was asked to verify the safety of GMOs. Pusztai's findings were that they were a severe health risk. When he reported his findings, he was horrified to find out they had already been on the market for two years. What ensued was a long battle for the truth to come to light. Pusztai was fired. He was not allowed to report his findings and had his data confiscated. Only through what seems like a miraculous series of events, the truth was made known, and public outcry stopped GMOs in Europe. Not in the United

---

[18] Dawn Gifford, *The Difference Between Open Pollinated, Hybrid and GMO Seeds*, Small Footprint Family, https://www.smallfootprintfamily.com/hybrid-seeds-vs-gmos, Accessed Feb 21,2019

States, however. It is estimated that 85 percent of what sold in our grocery stores contain GMOs. The genetic material in these products are unstable. They have caused tumors in rats. It seems the genetic material is so unstable it can interfere with the cells in the intestines and cause tumors. A GMO tomato is NOT a tomato. It may look like one. It may taste somewhat like one. But it is NOT created by God. Its "truth" has been tampered with. I am just using tomatoes as an example, wheat, corn, potatoes and other products have also been tampered with.

If I am freaking you out, I am sorry. I am freaking out along with you! But I haven't even gotten to the worse part of it! Next on the agenda, Genetically Modified Humans! I believe this is the final deception. THE Lie. The antichrist's deception. Author and filmmaker L.A. Marzulli believes the mark of the beast will be a genetic altering device. I think he is right. In Noah's time, humanity lost its humanity. Through interbreeding with angels, mankind was on the brink of destruction. (Remember the word for corruption was destruction.) I think we are going to see the same thing in the last days with genetic manipulation. In case you think this is a long way off…

In looking for material for this chapter I found an article on the website geneticliteracyproject.org. It is entitled, *Is Biotechnology Changing How Humans Evolve?* Here is a quote from that article "**After 4 billion years of evolution by one set of rules, our species is about to begin evolving by another. Overlapping and mutually reinforcing revolutions in genetics, information technology, artificial intelligence, big data analytics and other fields are providing the tools that will make it possible to genetically alter our future offspring should we choose to do so. For some very good**

reasons, we will."[19] The article goes on to say the changes will start with cures for diseases and then move on to non-disease related traits. Another quote, **"We already have the enhancement tools we need to alter the genetic makeup of our species. The science is here. The realization is inevitable. Timing is the only variable."**[20]

As Christians we have to realize how unethical this is. Even if, as it probably will, begin with "good things" like cures for diseases or birth defects. Do scientists really think they can play God with the seed of humanity? Well the answer is yes. They don't honor God. They worship their own intelligence. The world views are going to crash We have to understand the ethics of what is happening.

As we come to the end times, the attack on the seed, every type of seed, is increasing at an alarming rate. I believe it will continue until it comes to that final climax when the antichrist is revealed. Mankind will believe **the lie.** (Satan's age-old line "you will become like God") Genetic alteration will possibly make man immortal or capable of a longer lifespan. But will cause mankind to be unredeemable.

All seed is holy. All seed carries that divine blueprint that makes it truly God's creation. I believe that genetic engineering is wrong. It tampers with the essence of creation- God's design. Whether we are talking about our garden seeds, cross breeding different species of animals or humans. In a sense, that DNA is God's truth. It is God's truth programmed into the seed of His creation, whether it is a daisy or a hippopotamus. It is God's truth for the identity and purpose of each creature. The enemy's attack against the seed is an attack against God and everything that is good. DNA is a divine language, written by God. Removing that truth from creation is

---

[19] Jamie Metzl, *Is Biotechnology Changing the Way Humans Evolve?* May 3,2016, https///geneticliteracyproject.org/2016/0503/biotechnology-changing-humans-evolve/ accessed Feb.21,2019
[20] Ibid.

removing "The Word", the creator, from the creation. At the highest level it is removing the image of God from humanity. If humanity is no longer made in His image, are they human? Are they redeemable? When does creation stop being what God created? This is almost the stuff of horror films.

Man is not the originator of truth. We have to have a standard of truth outside of ourselves. In creation, the seed is God's truth. Morally the Word of God, the Bible is our standard, our plumb line. When we vary from God's standard we spin into chaos.

Earlier in the book, I talked about a Moody science video. There is another video called *Signposts Aloft*. I find this video both convicting and upsetting, but it is still one of my favorites. Dr. Moon has such a way of teaching truth using science. In this video, Dr. Moon uses his knowledge as a pilot and instrument flying to teach the importance of having a standard of truth outside of yourself. He explains how once a pilot flies into the clouds, he must know how to rely completely on his instruments. In a world all white, he cannot tell which way is up or down. He completely loses his bearings. His instrument panel is his life line. Dr. Moon plays the recording of a pilot who is requesting permission to descend through the clouds for an emergency landing. The pilot is not an instrument pilot. Within seconds of entering the cloud, he loses his bearings and goes into a spin. The radio control tower tries to give him instructions, but it is too late. The pilot crashes and dies. Dr. Moon explains that the pilot didn't know how to trust the instrument panel above his own instincts.

Dr. Moon sums it up so well I transcribed his closing words. **"On the instrument panel of every airplane and within every human heart and mind these words should be deeply etched, 'There is a way that seemeth right unto a man, but the end thereof are the ways of death.' without an accurate eternal standard of reference we can be completely wrong and not** even know it. The same thing can apply to reason and logic when faced with several equally logical alternatives, we can't just trust the way we feel. At such times man must have an accurate standard of reference to guide him.... This unshakeable faith that the universe is governed by unchanging laws is the cornerstone of modern science. Now there is just one area where man still clings to the outmoded idea that there are no absolute laws to guide him. This is the moral and spiritual, an area where man is making little if any progress, the one area where he refuses to accept a standard of reference outside himself. ... God has provided a complete system for our moral and spiritual guidance. He has given us a handbook which describes its unchanging standards..."[21]

We tend to separate moral and scientific laws into totally different categories, but the God who ordered the universe, who keeps the planets in orbit and holds the vibration of the atom in check, has given us the standards and boundaries for our lives and decisions. We cannot not honor Him in the church pew, while dishonoring Him in the test tubes and laboratories, or vice versa. God created everything and saw that it was good. When that creation is tampered with, is it not blasphemy? The seed of creation is holy, and the Word of God is holy. These are the standard of the creator.

"On the contrary, who are you, O man, who answers back to God? The thing molded will not say to the molder, 'Why did you make me like this' will it?" Rom.9:20

---

[21] Irwin Moon, *Signposts Aloft,* (Chicago, Il, Moody Publishers 2005)

Chapter 5

The Legal System of Spirit Realm

I am a visual learner. I have this picture in my mind of a puzzle. Every piece of truth is a piece of that puzzle. With each new piece, the whole picture gets clearer, and the next truth is easier to understand. I love these nuggets of truth. They are like precious gems to me. Especially the ones revealed to me in my own spirit, rather than just learned. But either way, I have this picture in my head of a giant puzzle of truth, and every now and then I get a new piece. I get so excited I think I am going to bust. I know what the whole picture is. I figured that out a while ago. I called my sister up on the phone, breathless with excitement.

"I figured out the secret of the universe!!!" I blurted into the phone.

"Jesus." she answered

"Yes, how did you know?"

Well, I guess it is obvious, but it was a new and fresh revelation to me at that moment. Every piece of knowledge, every truth (if it is real and not distorted or manipulated, which happens a lot, nowadays) leads us to a revelation of Christ. I mean all of it! The alphabet, math equations, science, seeds, water…. Everything points to Christ Jesus!

I had this great revelation after learning about the Hebrew alphabet. I first read about this in Chuck Missler's wonderful book *Cosmic Codes*. Then I ordered Frank Seekin's book *Hebrew Word Pictures*. The Hebrew alphabet started out looking quite different than it does now. It was a series of pictographs. Every letter was a picture that had meaning. So, every letter has both a phonetic sound and a picture concept. The words were not just a combination of sounds, but also a combination of ideas that describe the object.

The easiest example of this is the Hebrew word for father. It is AB. The letter for A looks just like our A, only turned on its side or upside down. It is a picture of an ox head. An ox was considered the strongest animal, so it represents strength. Ultimately the strongest of the strong is God, so it could represent Him also. The letter B is the floor plan of a tent. It means house, home, or in. So, the two letters together mean "the strength of the house", which of course is the father. When you combine the meanings of each letter, strength and house, it describes a father, while the letters form the word. Another simple word is EL, the singular word for God. It combines the A again, the strongest, with the L which is a shepherd's staff. The L means authority or power. As the shepherd's staff is a representation of his authority and power over the sheep, so the word for God, AL means the strongest authority, the strongest power.

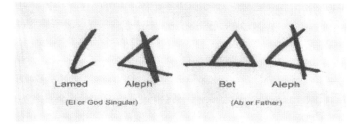

Lamed   Aleph   Bet   Aleph

(El or God Singular)   (Ab or Father)

Isn't that awesome? It started me on a journey of so many interesting words and ideas. I was looking at the Hebrew word for alphabet, which is alefbet. (The first two letters of the Hebrew alphabet.) The word alef takes the word for God, El, then adds a *pey,* (our p or f) which is the picture of a mouth, meaning to speak. The pictographs say *El* or *God speaks.* The letter *B,* in Hebrew is the word *bet.* This is also the word for house, but if you look at it, it contains the pictographs for house (*B)* and covenant

(*T*).

T △ ο ᒻ △

Bet-house
Tau-covenant or marker

Alef-strongest(ox head)
Lamed-authority (shepherd staff), El or God
Pey-speak (mouth)

God speaks to His covenant house.

If you read the meanings of the pictographs individually, the message of the letters says: "*God speaks to his covenant house*!!" Wow. That's what the alphabet is! That is what language is! God speaking to us! Then we have Jesus over in the book of Revelation saying: "*I am the Alpha and Omega.*" Alpha is the first letter of the Greek alphabet and Omega is the last. I know we take that to mean that I am the first and the last, which of course it does. But He is also saying I am the alphabet. And the alphabet is saying "God is speaking to His people." It reminds me of Hebrews 1:1 "*God after He spoke long ago to the Fathers and the prophets in many portions and in many ways, in these last days is speaking to us in His Son...*" The alphabet or language is in a sense a revelation of Jesus.

About this same time, I watched a YouTube video about a mathematician in the science of probability. He did not believe in God. On the video he had an equation that filled a white board. The equation demonstrated that what seems to be random, if you follow the math, leads to a definite outcome. Or in other words, there is no randomness. If that which seems to be random, actually has a definite outcome, then that outcome has to be determined by someone. The only possible person that can determine the outcome of everything is God! Math actually led him to believe in God! (Interestingly in Hebrew

75

the alphabet is also the numbers, so every number also has a meaning and every word has a numerical value.) While thinking about these things, I had the mind-blowing thought "All true knowledge leads to Christ and is a revelation of Him!" That is what prompted me to call my sister ecstatically that day and blurt out, "I've discovered the secret of the universe!"

"For since the creation of the world His invisible attributes, His eternal power and divine nature have been clearly seen, being understood through what has been made, so that they are without excuse." Rom. 1:20

All that I have written in these first few chapters are "pieces to my puzzle" that will help make sense to my topic. Another big piece of the puzzle is the legality or justice system of the spirit realm. This is very important toward understanding the legality of our redemption: that it was actually a legal transaction.

The challenge God had in redeeming mankind is He had to do it legally. Rom. 3:26b says *"so that He would be **just** and the **justifier** of the one who has faith in Jesus."* God had to do things justly. He can't close His eyes to sin and injustice or He would no longer be just Himself.

Isaiah 5:16 says *"But the Lord of Hosts will be exalted by His **justice**, and the holy God will show Himself holy in righteousness."* (Berean Study Bible) He is judge. He has to things legally. Jer. 9:24 says *"but let him who boasts, boast of this, the he understands and knows Me, that I am the Lord who exercises loving kindness, **justice** and righteousness on earth for I delight in these things declares the Lord."*

Just as a judge here on earth, would be considered unjust if he ignored the crimes of his own children, so God would be also. He cannot change His standards.

There is a legality in the spirit world, even more so, than in the natural. The name Satan means *adversary or accuser.* I looked up adversary also. It means: *one's opponent in a conflict, contest, or dispute.* In the courtroom of Heaven, there is one who is bringing accusation against us, Satan our adversary.

Job

There are several places in the Bible where we can take a peek into this heavenly court system. The first is in the book of Job.

Job 1:6-11 *"Now there was a day when the sons of God came to present themselves before the Lord, and Satan also came among them. The Lord said to Satan, "From where have you come?"*

Then Satan answered the Lord and said, "From roaming about on the earth and walking around on it."

*The Lord to Satan "**Have you considered** My servant Job? For there is no one like him on earth, a blameless and upright man, fearing God and turning away from evil."*

Then Satan answered the Lord, "Does Job fear God for nothing? Have you not made a hedge about him and his house? You have blessed the work of his hands and his possessions have increased in the land. But put forth your hand now and touch all that he has and he will surely curse you to your face."

The book of Job is considered the oldest book in the Bible, but no one knows exactly where it fits in the timeline. He lived to be 140 years old, which would put him close to the flood. In this passage we see the accuser coming before God. I don't like the translation *"have you considered my servant Job?"*. because it makes it sound like God is suggesting Satan consider Job. In the Hebrew there are two words used for the word considered. The first can be interpreted *put, place, set or appoint* and the second is *heart, inner man, determination or will*. These words are followed by a basic preposition that can mean *on, above, against*. A much better translation of this phrase would be: *have you set your will against my servant Job?* The adversary is coming to accuse Job. Notice what God says about Job. *"For there is no one like him on earth, a blameless and upright man, fearing God and turning away from evil."* That is quite a compliment! God is proclaiming him the most upright man on earth. (So, I think this is before God declared Abraham righteous by faith). The accuser is bringing a case against the most righteous man on earth (from God's own admission.) Apparently, he can't find a sin to accuse him of, but only an impure motive. Satan is suggesting Job is only serving God for what he (Job) can get out of it. Satan is essentially saying to God, *the only reason the most righteous man on earth (so therefore anyone, because this is the best you have got) is serving You is for what you will do for him.* I am elaborating, but Satan was saying that Job or mankind doesn't love you. They only love the blessings. If you take them away, they will curse you to your face.

I believe the Bible is the chronicle of our redemption and everything in the Bible is there for a purpose. I have never heard anyone else day this, but I believe Job's part in the story of redemption is to prove that man is redeemable. That a man, in this case, Job, would love God and serve Him simply for the reason that He is God and not for what God would do for him. If you read what all happened to Job, it wasn't any normal test or trial. It was devastation from every possible angle.

The adversary (my paraphrase of course) is saying *Mankind will never love you. They will only serve you if you give them what they want.*

And our dear friend Job proved Satan wrong! Job maintained that he hadn't sinned, which he hadn't. But he would not curse God. He proved, in my opinion, that at least one man would serve God, even when he got nothing out of it.

In any case, in the book of Job the curtain is pulled back and we can see a peek into the courtroom of heaven.

Joshua the High Priest

Another peek is in Zechariah 3:1-5.

"Then he showed me Joshua the high priest standing before the angel of the Lord, and Satan standing at his right hand to accuse him.

The Lord said to Satan "The Lord rebuke you Satan! Indeed, the Lord who has chosen Jerusalem rebuke you! Is this not a brand plucked from the fire?

Now Joshua was clothed with filthy garments and standing before the angel.

He spoke and said to those who were standing before him saying, "Remove the filthy garments from him."

Again he said to him, "See I have taken your iniquity away from you and will clothe you with festal robes"

Then I said, "Let them put a clean turban on his head." So, they put a clean turban on his head and clothed him with garments while the angel of the Lord was standing by"

Here in Zechariah 3 we have Joshua the high priest of Israel. Joshua came out of the Babylonian captivity with Zerubbabel, the remnant of the kingly line of David. They represented the king and priest in the newly formed nation of Israel. Because of their sin and idolatry, the nation of Israel had been taken into captivity over seventy years before. Now they are returning to resettle the land. Satan is accusing Joshua and the Lord rebukes Satan and clothes Joshua with the festal robes. Here is the heavenly courtroom accusation and a heavenly justification. The Lord rebukes Satan's accusation, based on the statement "Is this not a brand plucked out of the fire?' This means the Babylonian captivity was the just punishment and the punishment has been paid. The sentence is complete. Joshua and Israel are now justified. They have paid the punishment.

One of my favorite books, *Angels on Assignment* by Charles and Frances Hunter tells about Pastor Roland Buck who had angelic visitations in the late 1970's. In his first visitation, the angel Gabriel showed Pastor Buck a vision of Jesus returning to heaven from the grave. He sees this from the heavenly view point. He then shows Pastor Buck that this segment in Zechariah is not only about the high priest Joshua, but is prophetic of our high priest Jesus, when He rose from the dead, after paying the punishment for our sin. Just like 2 Cor. 5:21 says "*He made Him who knew no sin to be sin on our behalf, so that we might become the righteousness of God in Him.*"

Jesus and Joshua are the same name in Hebrew. They have just been translated differently. Jesus came before the Father bearing our sin, but He fully paid the price and made us righteous. He also was a brand plucked from the fire of judgement. Joshua the high priest in the book of Zechariah is the son of Jehozadak, which means "*Yahweh makes righteous.*"

Joshua and Zerubbabel are both types of Christ in this chapter. Joshua is a type of Jesus the high priest. Zerubbabel is a type of Jesus the King, descendant of David and rebuilder of the temple. In this brief peek into the courtroom we actually see two events. Joshua the high priest standing for Israel and Jesus the great high priest standing for all mankind. Joshua was brought out of captivity in Babylon after seventy years. He was taken out of judgement. It was completed. Jesus was crucified, and descended into hell. The debt was paid. It was complete. These are taken out of judgement, there is no longer any condemnation or guilt. The filthy rags are removed. The priestly robes are put on.

The Disciples

Another peek into this courtroom is not so visual, but I think we can see the same pattern. In Luke 22:31 Jesus, during the last supper with His disciples, tells Peter "*Simon, Simon behold, Satan has demanded to sift you like wheat, but I have prayed for you, that your faith may not fail…*" The word *demand* used in this verse means to *turn over completely or demand for trial.* The accuser had come before the Judge with accusations against the disciples. He has a case against them. He had demanded to sift them as wheat. (In studying this verse to write this book, I was surprised to find out that Jesus was referring to all of the disciples, not just Peter. The word "you" is plural.) Apparently, this whole transaction had already taken place. Jesus had interceded for the disciples. The disciples were going to be sifted, but because of Jesus' intercession they would make it through. Did Jesus want Satan to sift the disciples as wheat? No, it doesn't seem like it. He interceded for them. There was some type of legal exchange. Satan had some sort of legal foothold he could accuse them with.

End Time Saints

Our next example is in Revelation 10:12 "*Now the salvation and the power and the kingdom of our God and the authority of His Christ have come for the accuser* (prosecutor, complainant at law) *of our brethren has been thrown down, he who accuses them before our God day and night. And they overcame him because of the blood of the Lamb and because of the word of their testimony, and they did not love their life even when faced with death.*"

The word for *accuser* means a *complainant at law*. At this future event, Satan will no longer have access to the throne to accuse the brethren, but unfortunately, he will still have access to earth. I believe this is part of the process of Jesus taking back His authority over the earth. It appears that Satan is thrown out of the heavenly realms first. However, we see from this passage that Satan accuses us before God. He is constantly looking for a legal loophole, (through our ignorance or disobedience) to bring accusation and judgement against us.

Jesus

My last example goes back to the last supper or Passover. Jesus tells the disciples, "*I will not speak much more with you, for the ruler of this world is coming and he has (holds, possesses) nothing in Me.*"

Wow, what a statement. Jesus says "He has nothing in Me,". There is no compromise, self-will, nothing that Satan can accuse Jesus of. There is no case Satan can bring against Jesus. Satan is coming to accuse Jesus, but there is nothing He can use against Him!

God's Will verses Satan's Will

We see another important point here. Satan is the ruler of this world. Adam handed it over to Satan when he chose sin over obedience to God. 1 Cor. 4:4 calls Satan *the god of this world*. So many people say if God is good, why is there so much evil in the world? Well because we don't see God's will on the earth (unless we submit to Him and do it.) Earth is man's will. Man turned it over to Satan as his god. Man serves his own will and his own pride just like the devil did. As Frank Sinatra would say "I did it my way." How can we accuse God for what is going on down here? He gave us free will.

Jesus taught us to pray "*The kingdom come, Thy will be done, on earth as it is in heaven.*" We wouldn't need to pray that, if God's will was already being done. If we want God's will on earth, we have to **submit** our will to God. We have to pray for it. I am always amazed at us Christians. When we tell people how to get rid of the devil, we tell them "resist the devil, and he will flee." We left out a very important part of that verse (found in James 4:7) the first part says "***Submit therefore to God***…"   If our will isn't submitted to God, if we are in rebellion, resisting the devil will have no effect! The reason for this is… if we are not submitted to God, we are already in agreement with the devil. Our will must be submitted to God's will.

If I own a house, it is mine. I control what happens in my house. But, if I give my house to someone else, I no longer have the say or authority of what goes on there. If I go to the house, I have to knock on the door. I have to be invited in. Unless the new owner gives me the authority, I don't have it any more. God gave the "house" to man. He gave us free will. Man chose to serve Satan, he rebelled against God. Now we must **invite God's will** in our lives through an act of our will, and submitting our will to His. We must reject rebellion and Satan's authority.

Our salvation wasn't a simple fix. There were many complicated problems dealing with justice and the legality of our situation. In the book *Paradise the Holy City and the Glory of the Throne*, Rev. Elwood Scott is visited by a friend Seneca Sodi who has died and spent 40 days in heaven. Scott records the heavenly visits Seneca Sodi experienced. During Seneca Sodi's time in Heaven, he was given a scroll with the creed of the Elders he met in heaven. The creed is recorded in the book. Here is an excerpt from the section about the attributes of God.

"God is infinitely wise, always knows what is best, always adopts means which will best accomplish His purposes. That is wisdom; for wisdom is the art of turning to best account our knowledge. Both in creation and providence, God's wisdom is seen. His wisdom and His works everywhere confirm each other as being of God. No higher wisdom has ever been seen or known than God's wisdom in the plan of human redemption. It solves the problem of God's justice in justifying the believer in Jesus Christ." [22]

Wow. I read that years ago, but it still sticks with me. The highest wisdom that has *ever* been seen was

---

[22] Ibid. p.131

the wisdom God used to legally bring about our salvation.

This is where I am heading with this discussion. God had a big problem when He wanted to redeem mankind. He had to have a just cause to forgive them. He had to have legal entry into the affairs of mankind. He had to find a way to forgive their debt legally. How could God be fair, right and honest but still forgive our sin? How could He have the legal right to enter this world, when He gave it to Adam? These seem like impossibilities. I will get to that, but first I want to discuss another piece of the puzzle. Faith.

Chapter 6

Faith

I don't think the importance of faith can be overstated in the Christian life and understanding of spiritual principles. We are justified by faith. It is this very revelation, this statement, that in the year 1517 propelled the world from the Dark Ages into the Reformation. A monk named Martin Luther was pondering a scripture that troubled him and did not make sense. The verse was Romans 1:17. *"But the righteous man shall live by faith"*.

Luther did not care for this passage, as it did fit in with what he was taught, and what he believed. But when the truth of this verse finally dawned on his mind and spirit, it did so with such force and clarity that it changed the world! The world went from the darkness of religious oppression to the light of freedom in Christ. Luther wrote his ninety-five theses and a new day had dawned. What power is in those words, *"the just shall live by faith"!?*

Faith is vital to the Christian life. We cannot even become a Christian without it. Once we are saved by faith, we must continue to live a life of faith. Without faith it is impossible to please God. James tells us we ask for wisdom in faith, and that the prayer of faith heals the sick. Of course, when we say faith, we mean faith in God. Even more specifically faith in the faithfulness of God's word. Like I said, I don't think it can be overstated. As far as I can tell from 1 Corinthians chapter 13, the love chapter, the only thing that trumps faith is love. I know we have already discussed faith in the chapter on creation. Faith is the substance of our material universe. But I would like to look at faith in its application to our spiritual lives and the role it plays in our relationship to God and spiritual matters.

Faith is of the Heart

I talked in Chapter 3 about the connection between essence and substance in the spirit realm. In the spirit realm there is a connection between the heart and the outward reality that we do not see in our dimension. I would like to revisit that. Things that we think of as only abstract ideas have a reality and substance in the spirit realm. Maybe even a higher reality than the physical realm! The last verse of 1 Corinthians 13 says *"But now faith, hope and love abide these three; but the greatest of these is love."* What is faith, hope and love? Can we put them in a test tube and examine them? No, we can't. But this verse says they abide. They are going to last forever. They are spiritual realities. This present world is going to be destroyed. But these mysterious three are going to last forever. So, what is more real? While everything we do must start with an act of the will, it must be of the heart to really be spiritually effective.

I used to think that what **I do** was what mattered before God. I was trying to **do** right, but I just really didn't know how. I would push everything inside. If someone made me angry, I would think I can't be angry, I am a Christian. But I was still angry. I didn't know what to do with it. As long as I acted nice, I thought that was pleasing to God. I didn't realize stuffing all those bad feelings inside was just storing them (like Achan hiding the spoils of Jericho). It wasn't getting rid of them. It was still in my heart. Jesus taught about this in the Sermon on the Mount. He said what is in your heart is important. The Jews knew it was wrong to commit adultery. Jesus said if you even look on a woman (or man) with lust in your heart, you have committed adultery in your heart. Our heart is what matters. If our heart is pure, our actions will be too. It's the same with faith. Faith is of the heart.

Sometimes people hear a faith message and it doesn't work and they think it is wrong. One of the best faith sermons I have ever heard preached was by a guy on the internet, that wasn't even a Christian. Don't shoot me, but I think he might have been new age. He was talking about quantum physics and kind of turning it into a motivational course on success. He was talking about your beliefs creating your reality. He said something like Does that mean if you get up every day and say 'Every day I am prospering.' that you will be successful? Then he said what I thought was amazing. He said "Only if that is your core belief. It is what you truly believe that will change your life. If you are saying that on the surface, but deep down you think that nothing good will ever happen to you, it won't work!"

Christians listen these are words of wisdom. We can believe for stuff, healing, provisions whatever, but we have to deal with our core beliefs. Do we really know that God loves us? Do we know that we are forgiven? Do we know that we have right standing with God? Do we have unhealed wounds in our hearts that are screaming "nothing good is ever going to happen to you!" or any other number of other lies. We have to get to our hearts. Faith has to come from the heart. Faith isn't hearing a guy on T.V. making promises, if you send this amount God will do this for you. It isn't trying something out. It isn't saying something so many times you drive everyone around you nuts. Faith is your heart planting itself deeply into God, firmly onto a specific word or promise revealed in scripture to you personally. Faith is reaching through the veil to that unseen realm, grabbing ahold of God and saying this is my reality. **God's faithfulness to His Word is the ultimate reality.**

I remember hearing about a bible teacher whose son died. When he heard the news, he had all the normal emotions you would expect in a traumatic situation. They were trying to take over his mind. He pushed them back. His son had been prophesied over and it hadn't come to pass yet. He held on to that prophecy. He knew that it had to come to pass. He refused the grief and pain. He decided God's word for his son superseded even death. By the time he got to the hospital, his son was alive.

Portals

Faith reached in and pulled God's will from that realm to this. My working definition of faith in the life of a believer: *Faith is a portal that brings God's will from that spiritual dimension into this physical realm.*

Now if you're from my generation you might be saying "What's a portal?" Just ask a ten-year-old, they will explain it to you! A portal is a door, but the difference is, a portal connects two realms or dimensions that seem to have no access to the other, rather than just moving like in a house from one room to the next.

I remember when my son was about 5 years old. He was watching a "Hot Wheels" kids show. I asked him, "Why do they keep driving their cars into a tornado?"

My five-year-old son explained to me, "That's not a tornado. It's a portal. It takes them into another dimension."

Wow, that really freaked me out. I had read Mary K Baxter's book *Divine Revelation of Hell*. In this book, for about a period of forty days, the Lord took Mary on visits to hell. They would go out from the earth's atmosphere and enter into something that looked like a tornado. It was actually a portal into hell. **"At that, we began to go even higher into the sky, and now I could see the earth below. Protruding out of the earth and scattered about in many places were funnels spinning around to a center point and then turning back again. These moved high above the earth and looked like a giant, dirty type of slinky that moved continuously. They were coming up from all over the earth. "What are these?" I asked the Lord Jesus as** we came near to one. "These are the gateways to hell," He said."[23]

There seem to be bad portals and good portals. In 2 Kings chapter two, Elijah was taken into heaven by a whirlwind. (I'd call that a tornado.) It was a portal into heaven. I have heard a very reliable prophet talking about different geographical areas with portals to heaven. I believe this is similar or the same as an open heaven. An area can be affected in the spirit realm, by either great evil or great obedience. These acts give territory or authority either good or bad. I think of when Elijah was discouraged, he ran to a cave. Jezebel was seeking to kill him. Where did he go to meet with the Lord? - to Mt. Horeb which is Mt. Sinai where Moses met with God and received the Ten Commandments! You can see pictures of this cave online. Several people Ron Wyatt, Bob Cornuke and others have found and photographed the real Mount Sinai. It is also explained in the book *The Exodus Case* by Dr. Lennart Moller. It is a fascinating subject. You can see pictures of the cave Elijah ran to. But my point is, He went to a place that was special. It must have been an open heaven.

Jacob, also met with God and wrestled with an angel at a special place. It was the same location that he had the dream of the stairway to heaven. It was the location that he had his first encounter with God and made a covenant with God. Years before, Abraham had built an altar in the same place, at Bethel. It seems that Bethel was a place of an open heaven or portal.

Perhaps the most battled over portal of all time is Jerusalem. This is the place where Jesus will return and set up His kingdom. It is the location of Melchizedek's kingdom. It is where Abraham offered up Isaac. Later it became the capital of Israel and the location of the temple. It has been under attack for many centuries

---

[23] Mary K. Baxter, *Divine Revelation of Hell,* (New Kensington, PA, Whittaker House 1993) p.16

since. I traveled to the holy land many years ago, when I was fourteen. My sister and I were blessed to be able to go there on a tour. One thing I remember is that the Eastern or Golden Gate to Jerusalem was walled shut, apparently by the Turks in the Middle Ages. This was specifically done to stop the Messiah from entering Jerusalem. Even beyond that, a cemetery was placed in front of the gate. This was to ensure that the priestly Messiah, could not enter this gate without being defiled. This seems like an illustration of the entire warfare over this portal, this Holy City. Ground Zero of this portal or Holy Place was the temple itself. As we all know, it has been totally destroyed. When it is rebuilt it will be defiled by the anti-christ. We can see the warfare that takes place over portals.

Appointed Times

These are geographic portals. Times can also be a portal. The Jewish Festivals or Feasts are called *moeds* in Hebrew. This literally means an appointed time. It was a time set up for God and man to meet. These are times of open heavens. These are times God and man have set aside to meet one another. The feasts are celebrations that commemorate great victories. They represent great truths. They are prophecy in pantomime. And most of all, they point to Christ, who He is, what He did and what He will do. These special days are cycles of blessings.

Somehow because of the great victories on these days, heaven is closer to earth. They are set aside for meeting with God and revisiting past victories. Let's take the feast of First Fruits for example, many wonderful events took place on this day. Noah's Ark rested on Mt. Ararat, the children of Israel crossed the Red Sea, Israel ate the first fruits of the Promised Land, and Haman was defeated in the book of Esther. Most importantly Jesus was raised from the dead! All these happened on the Feast of First Fruits.

Most believers know the feast of Pentecost when the Holy Spirit fell on the believers, which began infilling of the Holy Spirit and the church age. What many may not be aware of was that this was already an established Jewish feast. It is called the Feast of Weeks or Shavuot. It commemorates God coming down on the mountain and giving the Torah to Moses. After his resurrection, Jesus told his followers to wait in Jerusalem for the Day of Pentecost. It was a time and a place. It was a divine appointment. A portal was opened! Of course, they did, they waited, they were in the right place at the right time. The Holy Spirit came like a rushing mighty wind. Thousands were saved and a power explosion took place in the disciples who were present!

Unfortunately, there always seems to be a negative side to these truths. One of the saddest days of Israel's history is the day the spies brought back a negative report. The whole nation refused the promised land because of unbelief. This day was said to be the 9th of the month of Av. This is now a day of fasting and mourning for the Jewish people. Many other catastrophes have happened on this day or in between the day of the 7-10th of AV. It was the day Solomon's Temple was destroyed in 587 B.C. The second temple was destroyed on that day in 70 A.D. In 135 A.D. on the 9th of Av, Rome killed over 500,000 Jews after the Bar Kokhba revolt.

More recent events that happened on that date. In 1290 the Jews were expelled from England, in 1309 the Jews were expelled from France. In 1492, the Jews were expelled from Spain. In 1941, the Holocaust began. All of these happened on the 9th of Av. This time seems to be an evil portal. Of course, evil portals can be closed through the finished work of Christ. There are many prayer warriors that have dealt with the evil strongholds over nations, cities, and individuals through prayer and intercession. These are examples of portals, both good and bad, that are connected to time rather than place.

My sister has told me of something I would consider another type of portal. She said any experience that you have had in God, you can have again. You can revisit in your mind or memory past experiences with God and have them again! I feel like I have experienced this to some degree. I remember some revival services that were so amazing. When some of us who had been there would talk about them, we could feel that same anointing. I think I need to do this more.

There was a particular brother at my church. He was a wonderful man and a joy to be around, but one thing about him annoyed me. He would always tell me stories about the wonderful things God had done, but he would tell them so often. it would get annoying. I think that I had heard them all many times. One time when he was again telling one of his stories, I was thinking and praying to God in my head. I said something like "Father, I love brother so and so, but is he all there? He has told me the same stories so many times, I am starting to think that there is something wrong with him."

Well, the Lord answered me! He said "He is rehearsing my goodness. Look at him. Have you ever seen him not full of joy?"

I had to answer "No."

God said, "That's because he is constantly rehearsing my goodness, even if it is the same stories over and over again. You would be happier if you did it too!"

Even our thoughts can be portals to God's joy!

Well, back to our topic of faith. I am going to make a working definition of faith. Faith is a portal. It gives God access to our lives. It gives us access to the spiritual blessings that Jesus has provided for us. Bro. Kenneth E. Hagin used to say (not a direct quote, just from my memory) 'faith will cause God to bypass everyone else and find you.' I believe, it is a portal. We can have faith in God or faith in the devil (fear). It works both ways. Both take hold of something unseen, visualize it and bring it into reality in this realm.

Jesus said "He who believes in Me, as the Scripture said, 'From his innermost being will flow rivers of living water.'" But this He spoke of the Spirit, whom those who believed in Him were to receive; for the Spirit was not yet given, because Jesus was not yet glorified." John 7:38 The word *believes* simply means: "to have faith." When we have faith in Christ, even we ourselves, become a living, spiritual portal through which the Holy Spirit can flow out to others.

Faith Causes Us to Receive

If you read through the New Testament aware of faith, you will be amazed. I mentioned before I went to Rhema Bible Training Center. I sat under some wonderful teaching about faith. It opens up your eyes when you understand that we receive God's provisions through the portal of faith. Look at the ministry of Jesus. What caused him to be amazed? The centurion's great faith.

Matthew 8:5-10 *"And when Jesus entered Capernaum, a centurion came to Him, imploring Him, and saying, 'Lord, my servant is lying paralyzed at home, fearfully tormented.*

Jesus said to him, 'I will come and heal him.'

But the centurion said, 'Lord, I am not worthy for You to come under my roof, but just say the word, and my servant will be healed. For I also am a man under authority, with soldiers under me; and I say to this one 'Go! And he goes, and to another 'Come!' and he comes, and to my slave, 'Do this!' and he does it.'

Now when Jesus heard this, He marveled and said to those who were following, "Truly I say to you, I have not found such great faith with anyone in Israel..."

Wouldn't it be wonderful to have so much faith that Jesus marvels? Apparently, the whole healing thing wasn't a question of it was hard or easy to heal, it was a question of could He find faith in people.

Another time Jesus was amazed by the faith of a Canaanite woman. Jesus and His disciples were in the area of Tyre and Sidon. A Canaanite woman began to cry out to Jesus to heal her demon possessed daughter. Jesus ignored her. When the disciples asked Jesus to do something, He answered that he was only sent to the house of Israel. The woman came and bowed down before Him asking for help.

"Then Jesus answered her and said, 'It is not good to take the children's bread and throw it to the dogs.'

But she said, "Yes, Lord; but even the dogs feed on the crumbs from their masters' table'

Then Jesus said to her, "O woman, your faith is great; It shall be done for you as you wish.' And her daughter was healed at once." Matthew 15:26-28

Jesus was only called to the nation of Israel. He was Abraham's seed. God's plan of salvation to the Gentiles had not been implemented yet. He came as a Jew to the Jews. He was not being mean. He was staying within the guidelines of His ministry. And yet because of this woman's faith, she pulled the power of God past those boundaries and to her daughter! Her faith moved God and she prevailed. I think this situation could also fall under the legal system of heaven. Israel had a covenant with God. This woman did not, but she brought a valid case before Jesus. Her faith accessed heaven and her prayer was answered.

This was among foreigners, yet when Jesus went to His own hometown there was no faith. *"And He could do no miracle there except that he laid His hands of a few sick people and healed them. And He wondered at their unbelief."* (Mark 6:5-6) Here He was among people who could have received every miracle they needed. But there was no faith.

When did Jesus heal somebody and didn't even know it?

In Mark 4:25-31 when the woman with the issue of blood accessed His healing power by her faith. Think about it. She initiated the healing. He didn't even know who it was. He just felt the power go out of Him.

It is impossible to please God without it. The just live by it. How many times throughout the gospels did Jesus say things like "your faith has made you well," or "be it done unto you according to your faith" or "oh you of little faith".

There is a principle that someone must believe God in order for His will to be accomplished on this earth. Faith in God gives God access. It breaks through the authority Adam gave to Satan and it gives God a portal of access into this earth and the affairs of man.

Hindrances to Our Redemption

1.   Our redemption could not come through the seed of Adam (or man). Adam died spiritually and passed that sin and death to all men, because he carried the whole human race.
2.   God had to follow justice. He had to be just and the justifier. Satan had a legal right to make accusation against mankind. God had to find a way to legally redeem mankind.
3.   He had to have the portal of faith opened. He needed someone to believe Him to open the door for the redeemer to come from the spiritual realm into the physical.

We have already seen how God dealt with the first obstacle. Jesus was the going to be The Seed of Woman. Looking back on this, we understand that this meant a virgin birth.

Next, He had to do this legally. We may never understand on this side of Heaven, what all it took for God to accomplish that, but we will be looking into it more.

Thirdly, I believe, God had to have a man, a special man with whom He is in covenant with. A man that would open the portal between the physical and the spiritual. A man of faith. I believe the Bible is the story of The Seed. He was first the seed of woman. And then the seed of an amazing man… named Abraham.

Chapter 7

Abraham

Abraham is an amazing character. He is the father or progenitor of the nation of Israel. He is designated as the carrier of the Messiah. He is the first man to be in a blood covenant with God. He is considered the father of the faith. He was the first man to be made righteous by faith. The Jewish people instinctively knew their special standing with God was based on their heritage as descendants of this great man.

Even the place of the righteous dead in Luke 16:22 was called Abraham's Bosom. In many accounts of Heavenly visitations, often those fortunate enough to have visited heaven tell of being greeting in Paradise by Abraham.

I'd like to look at two aspects of Abraham's life that I think were crucial to God's plan for our salvation. These two aspects form a legal basis for Jesus to come to earth as a man, and have the right to carry our sins. These two aspects are the blood covenant and faith.

The Blood Covenant

The modern world seems to have lost the knowledge of the blood covenant. It was an important rite in all primitive and ancient cultures. It was a sacred bond between two individuals that could be broken only by death. If one individual were to break the covenant, his own family was to hunt him down and kill him.

The blood covenant was utilized for three basic reasons. E. W. Kenyon outlines these reasons in his book *The Blood Covenant.*

"If a strong tribe lives by the side of a weaker tribe, and there is danger of the weaker tribe being destroyed, the weaker tribe will seek to 'cut the Covenant' with the stronger tribe that they may be preserved.

Second, two business men entering into a partnership might cut the Covenant to ensure that neither would take advantage of the other.

Third, if two men loved each other as devotedly as David and Jonathan, or as Damon and Pythias, they would cut the Covenant for that love's sake"[24]

A blood covenant was not to be taken lightly. It was irreversible. It could not be broken. We have nothing comparable in today's society. Marriage used to be considered a covenant that could not be broken, but not anymore.

The specific rites in cutting the covenant vary from society to society. Some have degraded into being repulsive. This is probably due to the degeneration of that society, but the blood covenant rites are similar in all cultures. They include some or all of the following: witnesses for verification and accountability, an animal sacrifice, two written copies of the covenant sometimes signed with blood and sometimes worn by each participant as an amulet, a cut and exchange of blood with the scar being an important mark of the covenant, exchange of names, exchange of clothing or weapons, sometimes an exchange of sons, and a covenant meal.

Once the two men or tribes were in covenant, all of their resources were at the disposal of the other. If someone were to attack or come against one member of the covenant, he was coming against both. Many times,

---

[24] E.W. Kenyon, *The Blood Covenant*, (Lynnwood, Washington, Kenyon's Gospel Publishing Society,1995) p.8

just the sight of the scar or other evidence of the covenant was enough to keep enemies at bay. If one covenant member were to be killed, the other would avenge his death. If he or his family had a need, the other would meet it. According to Kenyon, there was a saying among oriental people, "**Blood is thicker than milk**,"[25] meaning a blood covenant partner was closer and more faithful than your own siblings who were nursed by the same mother.

An example of this type of covenant is found in the book of Joshua chapter nine. Joshua and the army of Israel had just destroyed the cities of Jericho and Ai. The nearby kings knew they were in trouble. The Gibeonites devised a clever plan to save themselves. They dressed in tattered clothing and put worn out sacks and provisions on their donkeys. They convinced Joshua and the leaders of Israel that they were from a long distance away and asked to make a covenant with Israel. The leaders believed this false story and made a covenant with the Gibeonites to let them live. Three days later they realized that they had been deceived, but it was too late.

"The sons of Israel did not strike them because the leaders of the congregation had sworn to them by the Lord the God of Israel. And the whole congregation grumbled against the leaders. But all the leaders said to the whole congregation, 'We have sworn to them by the Lord, the God of Israel, and now we cannot touch them." Joshua 9:18-19

In just the next chapter, five kings of the Amorites gather together to destroy the Gibeonites. You would think this would take care of Joshua's problem for him. Just let the Amorites destroy the Gibeonites, but no. They are now covenant tribes. Israel must come to the aid of the Gibeonites. They are bound by the covenant to fight their enemies. This was the famous battle where the sun stood still. Israel won with a great victory.

---

[25] Ibid.

99

Skip ahead about 400 years. David is now the king of Israel. There has been a famine in the land for three years. David seeks the Lord to find out the cause of the famine. The Lord answers David that it is because King Saul, the first king of Israel, had broken the covenant and killed some of the Gibeonites. David has to find a just settlement to make things right.

"*Thus, David said to the Gibeonites, 'What should I do for you? And how can I make atonement that you may bless the inheritance of the Lord?*" 2 Samuel 21:3 The Gibeonites asked for the life of seven of the household of Saul. David had to comply. The covenant Joshua and the leaders of Israel had made over 400 years before was still binding. Violating the covenant had serious consequences. Even this covenant, made under false pretenses, had grave importance. It meant the difference between life and death to the Gibeonites and breaking it meant life or death to the Israelites.

My point is to demonstrate the importance of covenant, but I would like to take a rabbit trail here. Perhaps this passage is troubling to some. Why would God put a famine on Israel, especially years after the offense? Why would God want seven of Saul's family killed? How could a loving God make such a strange transaction? Is this consistent with the attitude of Jesus? Didn't He forgive the woman caught in adultery when the Pharisees wanted to stone her? Well let's try to look at this through the lens of some of the things we have just learned about.

First, God never wanted Israel to make this covenant in the first place. They made it presumptuously without consulting Him. Israel was outside of God's will in making this covenant. James 5:12 tells us God's opinion on the matter.

"*But above all my brethren, do not swear, either by heaven or by earth or with any other oath, but your yes is to be yes, and your no, no. **So that you may not fall under judgement.***"

Israel fell under judgement by making a foolish oath.

Secondly, we saw how Satan brings accusation against God's people in a courtroom setting. He is an adversary at law. He is a legalist when it comes to your destruction. I am only speculating here, but I think it is a reasonable assumption that this famine occurred because Satan brought an accusation against Israel that was valid. Why at this time? Well only God knows for sure, but I propose it was because Satan already had King Saul in his grasp. He was saving the offense for a more opportune time. David who was a good and godly king was now in power. Now possibly, Satan would have more reason to bring harm on Israel.

Thirdly, taking the lives of seven of Saul's children was not God's idea, it was the Gibeonites! How much better it would have been if they would have just told David "We forgive this debt. There has been enough bloodshed already." **That** would have been God's will. And **that** is what He is asking of us!!!! When we forgive others, we are taking away Satan's opportunity to bring accusation against them! We are taking away a foothold for destruction in their lives! As Christians we should have the heart of God toward people. The heart of God is that God isn't willing for any to perish. Sometimes, I think we think of God as our genie in a bottle. If someone does us wrong, we expect God to strike them with lightening or something. If someone is my enemy, then they should be God's enemy. We have that all turned around! The best way I can describe this is with something I think all parents will relate to. If one of your kids is fighting with the other, they always want you to take sides. They want to be the good kid and the other the bad kid. But you love them both. You want the best for them both. You just want them to get along and love each other. We are to have God's heart. His heart is forgiveness! God isn't going to pick up your offenses. He wants you to get **His** heart for that person. His heart for that person is for their good.

David was obligated by the covenant to avenge the death of the Gibeonites.

These are some Bible examples of the blood covenant.

God and Abraham's Covenant

The covenant between God and Abraham was not the type of covenant that was made for protection or a business deal. Their covenant was the type made between two friends that loved each other devotedly.

Isaiah 41:8 says *"But you, Israel, My servant, Jacob whom I have chosen, descendent of Abraham, My friend."*

The word for *friend* here would be more accurately translated *beloved.* It is taken from the word *"to love"*.

God and Abraham were bosom friends. They were covenant friends. Genesis chapters 15 and 17 describe the covenant rites between God and Abraham. We see an exchange of weapons when God promises to be Abraham's shield. A sharing of wealth, when He says your reward will be great. Abraham cuts a heifer, a goat, and a ram into two pieces and also sacrifices a pigeon and a dove. Normally, both covenant partners walk between the pieces, but in this case only God walks between the pieces while Abraham is in a deep sleep. The word for deep sleep here is *tardema*. It has a connotation of death. It is the same word used when Adam was in a deep sleep and God removed his rib to make Eve. Tardema can be divided into two words. *Tor:* meaning turtledove, which is a type of Christ, and *dahm* which means blood. This word for deep sleep is a type of the death of Christ.

When praying and asking God about the significance of this deep sleep Abraham fell into, I was reminded of the significance of death or a ritual death that separates one from his old life and identity, to be reborn into a new life. Abram the Babylonian no longer existed! He was now Abraham the friend of God. He was reborn with a new identity. He was now forever connected to God. He was God's covenant man and God's covenant nation. He had a new name, a new identity and a new purpose. He was no longer the same. He was a man whose identity was totally entwined with God and God's promise for a redeemer.

Baptism and Mikvah

This deep sleep is very like baptism for the believer. Baptism is our death and separation from our old identity. It is dying with Christ to the old creation and rising with Him as a new creation. At this point, our old identity as a son of Adam dies. We are now a creation born of Christ and His seed. I believe baptism is more than just symbolic. I believe that it is a physical act that has spiritual power.

The strangest and most wonderful baptism service I have ever been to was at a revival service with Rodney Howard Browne. At the time, my mom and sister lived in Florida and attended Carpenter's Home Church, while we lived in Michigan. My mom kept calling us at all hours of the night, after getting out of church. She would say "We are having Revival! You have to come! This isn't revival like they just call a series of meetings a revival. This is revival!" My husband and I had four young children at the time, but when my mom kept calling, we packed up the car and headed to Florida. We were not disappointed. The meetings were like nothing I had ever experienced. The climax, for us was the baptism service. Rodney Howard Browne is from South Africa. Many of the places he had ministered were full of witch doctors and demonic activity. He explained the significance of baptism was cutting off the old life. He also told how in those areas with lots of demonic activity, they can preach and have meetings without much demonic opposition, but as soon as they would announce a baptism service, there would be an intense spiritual battle. Rodney said the demons couldn't swim! They would stay in the water and folks would come up delivered!

This baptism service was like no other baptism service I have ever been to. They set up a large, above ground pool in the front of the church. Four or five people would get into the pool with a "catcher" behind each person. Brother Rodney would pray for them all at once from outside the pool. Those getting baptized would fall under the power of the Holy Spirit, into the water! The usher behind them would lift them back out. Even though we didn't attend that church, my husband was able to volunteer as an usher. He helped carry, literally carry, folks out of the pool and drag them on plastic laid all over the floor to an empty spot. It sounds crazy, and yet there was a holiness and an awesome presence of God. I had to leave early with the kids and get them to bed. My husband came in late, after I was already asleep. I was awakened when my husband came in, by a rush of the presence of God! It was overwhelming. Walter prayed for me and waves of power went through my body. It was cleansing me. For several days after that baptism service, the power of God was on my husband so strong, that I felt like I was going to fall whenever he walked by.

Another time that the power of baptism became evident to me was an incident that happened to my sister, Summer and my niece, Joy. A young woman whom they were acquainted with had some sort of traumatic run in with Satanists while camping. We never heard exactly what happened, but her boyfriend who was a backslidden Christian knew she needed deliverance. He rushed the young woman to my sister and niece to be prayed for. When she arrived, she was convulsing and her eyes were rolling back in her head. Summer and Joy were able to lead her to the Lord and to receive the baptism of the Holy Spirit, yet she was still manifesting demonic activity. She was still jerking and her eyes were still rolling back.

Summer felt impressed that they should baptize the young woman, but the boyfriend was so distraught that she needed to take him apart to settle him down. When Summer returned the Lord had impressed on Joy that they should baptize the young lady. Summer had a pool in her backyard. As she lowered the girl into the water, Summer felt a whoosh of the demonic presence leaving. When she raised her out of the water, the young woman was radiant! She praised the Lord totally delivered. I believe baptism is more than just a ritual! It has spiritual power and spiritual significance.

Romans 6:3-4 *"Or do you not know that all of us who have been baptized into Christ Jesus have been baptized into His death? Therefore, we have been buried with Him through baptism into death, so that as Christ was raised from the dead through the glory of the Father, so we too might walk in newness of life"*

Baptism is not just a New Testament thing. The Jewish people practiced a ceremonial washing for several different events. It is called *tevilah* (immersion) or *mikvah* (gathering of the waters). In an article on The Messiah Prophecy Bible Project website concerning the mikvah it states **"For the observant Jew, the mikvah personifies both the womb and the grave and consequently, rebirth. It is regarded as a pure unadulterated avenue of connection with God: and for that reason, it is a place where hope is reawakened and strengthened. The mikvah, therefore, plays an important role from preparation for marriage and Yom Kippur to the purification of menstruant women. Teviah (full-body immersion) marks a change of status from being tamay to tahor-ritually unclean (impure or unfit for the presence of God) to ritually clean. This is necessary because anytime a person is to come into the presence of God, they must come tahor (pure)."**[26]   If a Gentile converted to Judaism they

[26] Mikvah(Baptism):The Connection Between Immersion, Conversion and Being Born Again, ((The Messiah Prophecy Bible Project, https://free.messianicbible.com/feature/mikvah-baptism-the-connection-

were circumcised and immersed in the mikvah. This symbolized their new identity. Another use of baptism was in the Jewish wedding. I think this makes a beautiful illustration of the new birth. The bride was immersed in the mikvah before the wedding. This represented her purity and that she was set apart for her husband alone. Her old identity was changed. Her name was changed to that of her husband's. She was now a part of his lineage. She exchanged family lines. The children she would bear would be of her new identity. They would be her husband's and his family's seed. Marriage is a holy, blood covenant. There is a death to the old identity. As the Bible says the two become one flesh. They are a new family. Their relationship to their parents is forever changed. They are bonded together as a new family.

Another rabbit trail here. Our society has lost a true understanding of marriage. Marriage is a humble giving of oneself to another. We often hear of a fifty-fifty marriage, but that kind of marriage will never work. That attitude says I will put in as much effort as you, but no more. True marriage is laying down your life for your spouse, as they are. It isn't "I will love you, if you meet my expectations," That is self-centered. Even the marriage ceremonies of today seem out of whack to me. Yes, we should celebrate. Yes, family and friends should be a part. But what we see many times is kind of a "diva festival". It seems to be a self-centered meeting of the bride's every fantasy. Often the groom is swept aside in the obsession with the perfect dress and the perfect day. Many times, now the Maid of Honor is expected to throw showers and bachelorette parties. I have even heard of bachelorette cruises on an ocean liner! Some brides are not even willing to take the husband's name! How is any of this preparing the bride to lay down her identity and become one with her husband? Where is the humility? Where is the purity? Where is the separation to the

between-immersion-conversion-and-being-born-again/) accessed May 3,2019 husband? This isn't marriage. It is trying to make another person an extension of your own ego and identity. And when they no longer fulfill you… well you move on to the next person who makes you happy.

Several years ago, I was invited to the wedding of my friend's son. I had known this young man as a child, but had lost touch with him over the years. I had never met his fiancée. Yet at the wedding, from the very first sight of this young lady as she walked down the aisle, I was incredibly moved and knew this young man had chosen wisely. It was obvious that this lovely young woman's focus was on her love for her husband. She exuded humility and love. This day was not about her perfect princess dreams. It was about loving the man she was marrying. It brought me to tears! It was so beautiful. I found out later that she had had a mikvah the night before! That was the first time I had even heard of a mikvah, but the spirit in that wedding was one of godly love and humility. I believe this young couple will stand the test of time, because the foundation of the marriage was in dying to their own lives to become one!

This is what Abraham did. Although he was not baptized, this tardema sleep represented a death to his old identity. He became God's man. They were closer than blood family. Their identity was intertwined. He left everything behind and followed and believed God. This death to his old life is typified by the deep sleep. As Abraham was in this deep sleep, he saw a smoking oven and a burning torch pass between the carcasses. God walked through the pieces without Abraham. This represents that the covenant rested on the faithfulness of God alone. It is the same with our salvation. We cannot be faithful. Christ is faithful. Our part is to learn to die.

Exchange of Names

In a covenant there is often an exchange of names. In Abraham case, God does this when He changes the names of Abram and Sarai to Abraham and Sarah. In each case the Hebrew letter *Hey* (similar to our *H*) is placed in their names. The letter *Hey* is the fifth letter of the Hebrew alphabet. Five represents grace. God is putting His grace in Abram and Sarai's lives. It is also considered half of the name of God, YHVH. God is inserting part of His name into theirs. After this, God also referred to Himself as the God of Abraham, or the God of Abraham, Isaac and Jacob. The importance of this blood covenant cannot be understated. A man in covenant with a man of higher status has all the power and resources of his covenant partner available to him. Abraham has God as his covenant partner! God will never die. God has all power and resource available to Him. This covenant elevated Abraham to a status unknown to any other man on earth. He was God's man, God's covenant friend!

Abraham's Faith

My favorite television show is called *It's Supernatural.* It is hosted by a Jewish believer named Sid Roth. Every week I watch it on my computer. It has encouraged me through many hard times. I love Sid, although I have never met him. He is not ashamed of the Holy Spirit. He is bold and will obey God right in front of the whole world.

About twelve years ago I felt the Lord prompting me to pray in tongues an hour per day. I am ashamed to say, I just dismissed this nudging. "I can't do that. I just don't have the time." A few years later I was watching *It's Supernatural.* Sid and his guest challenged everyone to pray in tongues an hour per day. I knew I couldn't ignore it anymore. I started and did my best.

About six months later, I got up and was praying my hour. While I was praying, I had a question for God in my head. I was just kind of asking and wondering. When wham! I got a download from God. He answered my question with a whole teaching. I got scriptures and an explanation all at once. Wow! That was great. I began to notice other things. Mostly an awareness of my spirit. I used to have a very difficult time getting back to sleep, if I was awakened in the night. I would lay there for hours. But after this, I could just focus on my spirit (my belly) and immediately go back to sleep. I began to get more "downloads" of beautiful nuggets of truth from the Lord. They are like little treasures. I can think about them and get blessed all over again. (Some of them I have already written.)

Spiritual Rivals

One night I had some deep groaning and shouting while praying in the Spirit. I didn't know what it was about, I have a particular child who needs lots of prayer. I thought I must be praying for her. So that is what I figured it to be. Looking back now, I don't think so. First Corinthians 14:2 says about praying in tongues:

"For one who speaks in a tongue does not speak to men, but to God. For no one understands, but in his spirit, he speaks mysteries."

And that is what I think I was doing, speaking mysteries. The next morning when I woke up, just as I was waking, a thought came to me, not so much in words as in ideas. "You have always thought of Jesus and Satan as (and here is where I have a hard time finding the right word) eternal rivals (That's not expressing it exactly, but) the two engaged in the battle of the ages, the battle for mankind. But Jesus is NOT Satan's rival. Satan is no problem and no threat to Jesus.

I was shocked. I had never even questioned this. It was a totally new idea to me. My thoughts responded, "If it isn't Jesus, then who?"

"Abraham."

The words hit my spirit with huge impact. I was almost breathless. I can't really explain it. And yet the thought was so foreign to me, I was afraid to write it down. I was afraid it was heresy or something.

The thoughts continued. God had no problem with Satan. He is totally insignificant in comparison to God. Man. Man had a huge problem. Man had the problem with Satan. And man was totally incapable of dealing with him.

Yes, Jesus conquered Satan. Jesus destroyed his power and authority over mankind, but He did NOT do it as God, the Eternal Word.

He did it as a man.
He did it as the seed of Abraham.

I figured I better study this out. I studied the verses about Abraham. I found this to be true. I found what Abraham believed. What he had faith for, and I was amazed.

Did you ever wonder about how the Bible says in Romans 4:3 *"For what does scripture say? Abraham believed God, and it was credited to him as righteousness."* I used to wonder about this. Although believing God for a child when you are unable to have one is good and honorable, why did that faith make Abraham righteous? Didn't Hannah, Samson's mother, Rebecca, Rachel, Elizabeth all have children after being barren? But their faith wasn't credited to them as righteousness. Why Abraham? As I studied, I found out what Abraham actually had faith for. He wasn't just having faith for **a** child. He had faith for **the** child. The Child, The Messiah, Jesus.

Abraham's faith was for Jesus to be born, become an innocent sacrifice and be raised from the dead!   It was also for a heavenly city to live in!   Abraham's faith was in Jesus.   Abraham's faith (orchestrated by God) opened the door, the portal. Jesus now had legal access by faith to come as Abraham's seed. He had access to redeem the world. Abraham was justified **by faith in Christ**, his seed!

Faith Review

Let's review faith a little here. Mark 11:23-24 (our primer on faith) says *"Truly I say to you, whoever says to this mountain, 'Be taken up and cast into the sea' and shall not doubt in his heart, but believes that what he says is going to happen, it will be granted to him. Therefore, I say to you, all things for which you pray and ask, **believe that you have received them and they will be granted you."***   The thing that is so easy to misunderstand about faith is, you have to believe that you have what you say *first* before anything has changed. Then it is granted. The word for granted there means: To be or exist. You receive it when you believe it, before it is actually a physical reality. Then the faith pulls it into being, into reality. The faith **IS** the substance of what is hoped for. Abraham's faith was the title deed to Messiah coming. Abraham believed for a Savior, not just for himself. At first Israel, his physical seed, inherited his blessing and covenant. Then later the mystery was revealed. We all got to get in on "the blessing". We are blessed with Abraham the Believer. As Abraham's spiritual seed we inherit the blessing.

Galatians 3;6-9 says *"Even so Abraham believed God, and it was reckoned to him as righteousness. Therefore, to be sure that it is those who are of faith who are sons of Abraham. The Scripture foreseeing that God would justify the Gentiles by faith, preached the gospel beforehand to Abraham saying "All the nations will be blessed in you" So then those who are of faith are blessed with Abraham the believer."*

Abraham believed for Jesus. He believed and was made righteous, because his faith brought Christ. Abraham's faith was future tense. We believe in Jesus. We are made righteous by believing in what Jesus has done for us …. past tense…. We join with Abraham in faith. Really, I am saying past tense and future tense, because we are in this timeline of events. But Abraham's faith went outside of time and made Jesus' redemption a reality. Our faith goes outside of time too. It goes into the eternal realm. It unites us to Jesus and His death and resurrection. It unites us to Abraham and makes us his children.

Let's look at what the Bible says Abraham believed for. He believed God for a supernatural or impossible birth, he believed God for a heavenly city, and he believed God for the resurrection of the dead.

Abraham Believed for a Supernatural Birth

First, a supernatural birth. Abraham was the carrier of Messiah. God said in your Seed all the nations of the earth will be blessed. It was an impossibility for that Messiah to be born, because Sarah was barren and both were past child bearing age. Abraham carried the Seed. In a sense Isaac was the "proxy" for Messiah. Where was Jesus the man? Not the eternal Jesus in heaven, but the physical genetic DNA that would become his physical body? It was in Abraham and it was in Isaac. But in a sense, the Seed of Messiah was dead! Without Isaac's birth there would be no Christ, the man. But Isaac's birth was impossible. If you know the story, Sarah was barren. It was impossible for her to have a child. And beside that she was past the age of having children. She could no longer just be healed of whatever was wrong. It was too late. The New Testament seems to indicate that Abraham body was also "as good as dead" in regard to bearing children. It was a birth that **had** to be supernatural, just like a virgin giving birth. It is an impossibility. Abraham was believing for a birth that could only be supernatural. Romans 4:16-24 *"For this reason it is by faith in order that it may be in accordance with grace, so that the promise will be guaranteed to all the descendants, not only to those who are of the Law but also to those who are to the faith of Abraham who is the father of us all (as it is written, "A father of many nations have I made you.")* (You see Abraham has two kinds of children, physical children and spiritual children, if you have been born of faith, you are Abraham's spiritual seed) *in the presence of Him whom he believed, even God **who gives life to the dead and calls into being that which does not exist.*** (God gave life to the dead seed in Abraham and called into being The Seed of first Isaac, but ultimately Jesus the Man). *In hope against hope, he believed, so that he might become a father of many nations according to that which had been spoken, "so shall your descendants be." without becoming weak in faith he contemplated his own body now as good as dead since he was about a hundred years old, and the deadness of Sarah's womb; yet with respect to the promise of God, he did not waver in unbelief but grew strong in faith giving glory to God and being fully assured that what God had promised, He was also able to perform. Therefore, it was credited to him as righteousness,* (Abraham's faith caused Jesus' the SEED to live! That SEED was Abraham's salvation and redemption. He, Jesus the Man, was now a done deal...the faith was exercised. He was coming! That is the basis of Abraham's righteousness...faith in Christ!) *now not for his sake only was it written that it was credited to him, but for our sake also, to who it will be credited as those who believe in Him who raised Jesus our Lord from the dead."* We enter into Abraham's faith when we believe in Jesus.

The phrase "**who gives life to the dead and calls into being that which does not exist**" summarizes what Abraham believed for. According to this verse he had to believe for a supernatural birth from both sides, his and Sarah's. Abraham believed for The Seed that was now dead inside of him to be made alive. And Sarah's body which did not have the ability to produce to conceive. This was in proxy for Mary's supernatural birth.

Just as a side note: Sarah thought she was disqualified from carrying and giving birth to The Seed, because she was barren and too old to have a child. In her culture a woman's job was to bear a son. Much of a woman's self-esteem in those days was in her ability to produce that child. I don't think it is a stretch to say that not being able to have children was Sarah's greatest disappointment in life. Maybe so much so that her identity was affected, her feelings of value and self-worth. Now God is saying that she will be the mother of many nations! The one thing she is incapable of doing. So, she did what she felt was noble. She made the ultimate sacrifice that she could make as a wife. She was willing to share her husband with another woman. Can we get a little human here? I think the idea was as painful to her as it is to us. She lived in a culture where a man could divorce his wife for not having a son. Or maybe he would just get another wife to do it. She had a faithful man. He didn't do that. He was willing to live without a child, rather than dishonor Sarah. She was willing to sacrifice, but God didn't want her sacrifice. God wanted her faith. I have had places in my life that I "sacrificed". It didn't turn out any better than Sarah's situation. Sacrifice leads to self-righteousness, which leads to pride and a judgmental attitude. It all stinks. It was Sarah's *barrenness that qualified* her to carry 'The Seed". It had to be a faith child. It had to be impossible. They were actually believing for Jesus' impossible birth. Isaac was a type of Christ. Isaac carried Christ in his loins, just as we learned about how Levi paid tithes while he was in the loins of Abraham. And we died

114

spiritually while we were in the loins of Adam. Jesus was in the loins of Abraham. Jesus was dead, in the loins of Abraham! (I mean His physical DNA). His birth was impossible. The first thing that we see Abraham believed God for was a supernatural birth.

Abraham Believed for a Heavenly Home

Secondly, Abraham believed God for a homeland. We know that Abraham left his homeland and stayed in Canaan as a nomad. He lived in tents and moved about at times. God promised him that land for his inheritance. We think of Abraham as believing for the land of Israel. And I think he did, but it goes beyond that. Hebrew 11:8-19 tells us what Abraham believed God for. Verse 10 is quite a surprise. It says "for *he was looking for a city whose architect and builder is God."* And verse 16 goes on to say *"But as it is, they desire a better country, that is a heavenly one. Therefore, God is not ashamed to be called their God for He has prepared a city for them."*

Abraham believed God for heaven! That makes me think of the story in Luke 16 about Lazarus the beggar who lay at the rich man's door. When he died, he went to Abraham's bosom. Both Jesse Duplantis and Seneca Sodi in their experiences in heaven, talk about meeting Abraham. He greets the new comers. They both mention Paradise as being Abraham's bosom. Wow again. Abraham is quite a guy! I'd say he is quite a pivotal person in the redemption story! Let's see what else Abraham believed God for.

Abraham Believed for Resurrection of the Dead

And lastly, Abraham believed for the resurrection of his only begotten son. Remember how Levi paid tithes inside of Abraham's loins? Jesus was now in Isaac. (His lineage, the family tree of Mary.) All of the promises God

115

made to Abraham hinged on Isaac. It was now in Isaac that The Seed would come. It was in Isaac that all the nations of the earth would be blessed. God told Abraham to go on Mount Moriah and sacrifice his only begotten son. Abraham was willing to do this.

Hebrews 11:17-19 tells us why. *"By faith Abraham, when he was tested offered up Isaac, and he who had received the promise was offering up his only begotten son. It was he to whom it was said 'In Isaac your descendants shall be called.' He considered that **God is able to raise people even from the dead, from which he also received him back as a type**."* Abraham believed for his Seed to be raised from the dead!!!! That's Jesus we are talking about!

Wow!!! No wonder Abraham's faith was reckoned to him as righteousness. Abraham's faith was in Jesus. Abraham believed for him to be born of a supernatural birth, to be raised from the dead and for a heavenly city!!!! Abraham's faith brought Christ to earth! It was a done deal. He had to come. I can't wait to get to heaven and give him a big hug. Let's also not forget about the blood covenant and its significance in Abraham offering up Isaac as a sacrifice. Remember a blood covenant partner had all the resources of his counterpart at his disposal if he needed them. God called upon Abraham, his beloved friend, to honor their covenant relationship by offering up his only begotten son. Abraham's willingness to do this gave God the legal right to reciprocate and offer up His only begotten Son.

So, we have several things happening in this one crazy faith act of Abraham's! He is proving the strength of the blood covenant between he and God. He was willing to offer up that one thing in life that was dearest to him, his only son.   Secondly, he was believing for a resurrection of the dead, because he knew every promise God had given him would be accomplished through Isaac. If he killed Isaac, God would have to raise him from the dead in order to fulfill His promises. Thirdly, when he was believing God for Isaac to be raised from the dead, he was also believing for Jesus to be raised from the dead! This is through that same principle of seed. Jesus (his physical DNA) was present in Isaac's loins as he was being offered up as a sacrifice. Jesus the seed of Abraham would have died, His birth would have then been an impossibility. Just as if your father would have died as a child, you would not exist. So, in a sense, Abraham not only believed for Isaac to be raised from the dead, he believed for Jesus to be raised from the dead.

From Adam to Abraham, mankind and the earth were in the grasp and authority of Satan. Now something new was on the earth-a rival, a threat to Satan's plan. He was a man of God's own possession, kindred blood joined friends. Not only that, he was a seed. A seed that would bring forth that ultimate Seed. The Seed God had promised. The Seed in whom the whole world would be blessed.

Let's follow The Seed through the Bible. First, we see He is "the Seed of woman". Then we see Satan trying to destroy the seed of all mankind (therefore women) by corrupting the DNA with fallen angels and animals.

Now we see the Seed is in one man's line, Abraham. Do you see how Abraham is now the rival of Satan? Here is a man with a covenant with God. Man is no longer helpless and hopeless. Abraham is righteous. He has been raised up against the tyrant Satan. His heirs, the nation of Israel, have too. They are Satan's foes, his rivals. Isaac's birth was the birth of a nation. When I pondered this thought, I realized that Israel was pregnant with the Messiah. By faith He was coming. By faith, He had to come. I thought: "Is there a Bible verse that says this?" Then it hit me. Revelation 12:11 *"A woman clothed with the sun and the moon under her feet, and on her head a crown of twelve stars, and she was with child..."* Here we see Israel depicted as a woman who gives birth to Jesus. Abraham and his physical seed

117

are the opposition to Satan. They are the rivals fighting for this planet.

Jesus our Hero, our Savior, did not come to earth as God.

He came to earth as man ...the child…. The Seed of Abraham.

"For assuredly He does not give help to angels, but He gives help to the descendent of Abraham." Hebrew 2:16

Chapter 8

Following the Seed

Following the Seed through the generations is like following heroes of faith. The Seed seems to follow those who had regard for it, those who contended for it by faith. And let's not forget the women. For every man that carried the Seed, there was a woman who did also.

Ultimately it was only a woman, Mary, that would say *"Be it done unto me according to your word."* Ultimately only a woman could carry Messiah.

From Eve to Mary there was a line of women who carried the Seed. In particular, four women are specifically mentioned in Jesus' genealogy in Matthew chapter one. Why were those four mentioned? I have heard it was to show that God could redeem even a colorful past. Three of these women were involved in some type of sexual impropriety and the fourth was a Moabite. The Moabite women were the ones who led the sons of Israel astray in the days of Balaam, and yet here one shows up in the genealogy of Jesus. Why are these specifically mentioned? Is it to demonstrate the power of redemption? Well, that is what I have been taught, and I believe it is true, but only as a by-product of the primary reason. The primary reason was these women, along with many of the men in the genealogy of Christ, **contended** for the Seed with faith. They honored the Seed. Let's look at some of the men and women who honored the Seed.

Jacob

Of all those who contended for the Seed, none of them seemed to do it with as much passion as Jacob. Although we can't always condone his methods, Jacob had an understanding of the value of carrying the birthright and blessing of God.

Even before Jacob was born, it was prophesied that *"the older would serve the younger."* The Bible just gives us the narrative of what happened. It doesn't tell us what should have happened. This story can be uncomfortable. From the surface it seems that Jacob was blessed for doing wrong. It seems like God was showing favoritism.

Love and Hate

I don't think that is the case. It is just that we are looking at the narrative through the natural eye. Let's look at another troublesome Bible passage. Romans 9:12-13 *"It was said to her, 'The older will serve the younger.' Just as it is written, 'Jacob I loved, but Esau I hated.'"* I really can't imagine God hating anybody. I don't think He does. The Bible says God is love. It also says God is light. In 1 John it says, *"He who hates his brother walks in darkness."* We know that God doesn't walk in darkness or act outside of love. I am guessing this Bible verse doesn't set right with you, either. I looked up the words used in this verse. This is what I found.

The word for love is *agapao.* This is the word we use for *the God kind of love*. It is defined *"to prefer, involving choice or selection."*

The word for hate is *miseo*. It is defined **"properly to detest on a *comparative* basis, hence, *denounce*, to love someone or something less than someone (something) else, i.e. is to renounce one choice in favor of another. [Note the comparative meaning of miseo which centers on moral choice, elevation one value over another]"[27]**

This is the same word used in Luke 14:26 *"If anyone comes to Me and does not hate his own father and*

[27] Helps Word Studies, (1987,2011, Helps Ministries Inc.)
https://biblehub.com/greek/3404.htm

mother and wife and children and brothers and sisters, yes and even his own life, he cannot be my disciple."

We can see from this verse the word hate means choosing a priority and not ill will. The Bible commands us to *"Honor your father and mother."* It commands us to love our wives, children, brothers and sisters. We are not talking about hate in the sense of wishing bad on someone. We are talking about choices and priorities.

Jacob's Love for the Covenant

So back to our verse *"Jacob I have loved, but Esau I hated."* God is talking about who is chosen to receive the covenant. Which son would carry the Seed? If we study the story of Jacob and Esau in Genesis chapters 25-27, we will see that Esau had no regard for the covenant or the Seed. The Bible said he **despised** his birthright. He sold it for a bowl of lentil stew. We can also see that he had little value for it in his choice of wives. He chose Canaanite wives. They were Hittites. Although she may have had ulterior motives, I don't think Rebekah was lying when she said, *"I am tired of living, because of the daughters of Heth."* speaking of Esau's wives.

There was only one man who had the privilege of cutting a covenant with the living God, of being declared righteous or in right standing with God. Abraham carried the beacon of hope for all mankind. It was an honor and a duty. The Seed was in jeopardy in the loins of such a man as Esau, a man with no regard or value to the special relationship Abraham and Isaac had with God. And he never did carry the seed. Even in the womb, God seeing all time, knew to entrust the seed with Jacob.

Jacob did value this honor more than anything else. Jacob's faith in the blessing and birthright of His father seemed to be the motivating factor of his life. His methods weren't necessarily right. He deceived his father, in order to receive the blessing. With the help of his mother he disguised himself as Esau, placing the skins of goats on his hands.

"*Then Rebekah took the best garments of Esau her elder son, which were with her in the house and put them on Jacob her younger son. And she put the skins of the young goats on his hands and on the smooth part of his hands part of his hands and on the smooth part of his neck. She also gave the savory food and the bread which she had made, to her son Jacob*" Genesis *27:15-17*

Jacob reaped what he sowed. He had the same case of mistaken identity in his own life with his wives. This time the older pretended to be the younger with the help of her father! When Jacob had worked seven years to marry Rachel whom he loved, his father-in-law pulled a switch on him. When he woke up the morning after the wedding, he found that he had actually married Leah the homely older sister. He had to work another seven years to "earn" the right to marry the woman he loved. He lived with rival wives because of it. Leah, the unwanted wife, carried the child Judah, who would carry on the line of Messiah.

Jacob a type of Christ

To take a detour from our topic of following the Seed through the line of Abraham, I would like to stop for a moment and look at a *type* of Christ. A *type* of Christ is a person or even an object in the Old Testament that represents Christ and shows us a little snapshot of truth about Christ and God's plan. I am a visual learner. I love types. Often, I can understand concepts much better from the Old Testament type.

Some examples of the types of Christ are: Adam, Abel, the Ark, Isaac, Jacob, Joseph, and Gideon. Studying types of Christ is fascinating. But for right now let's take a look at Jacob and Esau. Jacob is a type of Christ and Esau is a type of Adam. It is interesting that Esau's nickname, Edom, is almost identical to the name Adam. It has one extra letter but both have the same meaning, which is *red, corporeal one, dustling*. Esau and Adam were both the "first born". They both sold their birthright for a bite of food. The Bible says the older will serve the younger. Jacob was the second born. Jesus was the second Adam. Both became greater than their brothers. Jacob went on to be the nation of Israel which has an everlasting covenant with God. Esau became the kingdom of Edom which no longer exists. Adam's line was doomed to death, while Jesus line is going to everlasting life. When Jacob presented himself before his father, he took on the identity and "flesh" of his brother. Rebekah "*put the skins of the young goats on his hands and on the smooth part of his neck,*" to give Jacob skin like Esau's. He received the blessing from his father and saved the race of God's covenant people from the careless hands of Esau. Jesus came with the identity and flesh of Adam.

"...*Therefore, He had to be made like His brethren in all things, so that He might become a merciful and faithful high priest in things pertaining to God to make propitiation for the sins of the people.*" Hebrew 2:17

He presented himself before the Father as a man. He received the declaration that the debt of sin was paid from the guilt of Adam. The *older line* of natural man will give way to the *younger* (or new) lineage of Christ. That is the born-again race. "*Older serves the younger.*" That phrase is prophetic first of Jacob and Esau, but also, of Adam and Christ.

Back to the Seed

So back to following the seed. The seed goes from Abraham to Isaac (who is a type of Christ). It then goes to Jacob (who is a type of Christ). Where does it go next?

In "the hall of faith chapter" Hebrews 11:20-21 we read, "*By faith Isaac blessed Jacob and Esau even regarding things to come. By faith Jacob, as he was dying, blessed each of the sons of Joseph and worshipped, leaning on the top of his staff."*

That confused me. Why does it just mention Joseph and his sons, instead of all Jacob's sons? I thought the birthright went to all twelve sons.

Then I found the answer in 1 Chronicles 5:1-2. *"Now the sons of Reuben the firstborn of Israel (for he was the firstborn, but because he defiled his father's bed, his birthright was given to the sons of Joseph the son of Israel; so that he is not enrolled in the genealogy according to birthright. Though Judah, prevailed over his brothers, and from him came the leader, yet the birthright belonged to Joseph.)"*

Jacob was bypassing Reuben (the oldest again) because of his sin and giving the birthright to Joseph. And then he takes it a step farther and adopts Joseph's two sons, Ephraim and Manasseh, as his own. He is skipping a generation so his grandsons become like his sons. Each receive a blessing and become a tribe of the 12 tribes of Israel. Then he bypasses Manasseh, the oldest and blesses the younger, Ephraim, as the firstborn! Wow. There is a pattern here. Maybe Jacob had a revelation that this was prophetic of Jesus. Maybe he was just following the leading of the Lord. I don't know, but three generations of the birthright went to the younger son. This is why Ephraim is often equated with the whole nation of Israel in prophecy.

Judah

Although Ephraim carried the birthright, if you know your Bible you know he did NOT carry the seed of the royal line or Israel or the Messiah. God seems to have a different choice. Judah.

When Jacob blessed all of his sons at the end of his life, he blessed Judah saying, *"Judah your brothers shall praise you: your hand shall be on the neck of your* enemies; *Your father's sons shall bow down to you. Judah is a lion's whelp; from the prey, my son, you have gone up. He couches, he lies down as a lion, and as a lion who dares rouse him up? The scepter shall not depart from Judah, Nor the ruler's staff from between his feet, until Shiloh comes, and to him shall be the obedience of the peoples. He ties his foal to the vine, and his donkey's colt to the choice vine; he washes his garments in wine, and his robes in the blood of grapes. His eyes are dull from wine, and his teeth white from milk".* (Genesis 49:8-12)

Let's look at a couple of these phrases. "*Your father's sons will bow down to you.*" Does that sound familiar to you? It does to me...Joseph's dream. What Joseph lived in a type as the Messiah- Judah will become. I haven't really explained Joseph as a type of Christ. It is a great study and probably the most in-depth type in the Bible. It is too in-depth to get into at this point. This prophecy or blessing of Jacob to Judah seems to make reference to the fact that Judah's descendent will become the ruler that Joseph's life typified, namely Jesus.

"*The scepter shall not depart from Judah, nor a ruler's staff from between his feet, until Shiloh comes...*" Judah's line will be a line of kings until Shiloh or Jesus comes as the ultimate King.

"*And to him shall be the obedience of the peoples*" *This* verse is also translated "*And to him shall the gathering of the people be.*" Either way it is talking about Jesus. Every knee will bow and confess Him as Lord, or if the correct rendering is "*the gathering of the people*" it could be a reference to the rapture.

"*Judah is a lion's whelp...*" The Lion of the tribe of Judah is clearly Jesus (as it is written in Revelation 5:5).

"*He washes his garments in wine, and his robes in the blood of grapes.*" The footnote in my Bible says this refers to the prosperity in the millennial kingdom with wine being as abundant as water, but when I read it, I think of Isaiah 63. This is a chapter about the warrior Jesus. He returns with red garments from treading the winepress of the wrath of God. *"Why is your apparel red, and Your garments like the one who treads in the wine press?"* Isaiah 63:2

We think of the loving side of Jesus: Jesus the healer, Jesus our Justifier, but one day there will be a terrifying Jesus.

I live in a tourist town on Grand Traverse Bay of Lake Michigan. Every few years, we are visited by the Blue Angels. The Blue Angels are the U.S. Navy's flight demonstration squadron. My town loves the Blue Angels. We look forward to them coming. The sky is filled with a roar. For about a week before the air show, we see them practicing as they zoom across the sky. Cars pull over to the side of the road and just watch. The speed and precision and just raw power and accuracy of these planes and their pilots is awe inspiring. We love it. But I have often had the thought, 'What if these planes weren't here for an airshow? What would it be like if you were in a war situation and they came against you?' These planes that cause our town joy and excitement would be absolutely terrifying. They are so fast you could not get away from them or have enough warning to get to safety. Our beloved Jesus is a rock of safety for us. But if you were His enemy, well you just don't want to be. The Blue Angels would look like toys next to Him. Psalms 2 talks about this warrior Jesus also.

"Do homage to the son, that He not become angry, and you perish in the way, For His wrath may soon be kindled. How blessed are all who take refuge in Him!" Psalm 2:12

The lineage of Judah is the Messiah, Jesus, **The King of Kings.**

Why Judah?

Are you wondering like I was, why Judah? He did not seem to be special. The only redeeming thing he ever seemed to do was offer himself up in Benjamin's place. If you know the story of Joseph, after Joseph became ruler of Egypt, he tested his brothers. His brothers came to him for food during a famine, but didn't recognize him. Joseph put his own cup in Benjamin's sack. Benjamin was his full brother. The only other son of Rachel. Joseph arrested Benjamin to see if his brothers had changed. Judah offered his life for Benjamin's. This is when Joseph revealed his identity to his brothers. Beyond this, Judah didn't seem to have too many redeeming qualities.

Judah and Tamar

In Genesis chapter thirty-eight we have the strange story of Judah and Tamar. It is like one of those skeletons in the closet kind of stories. No one quite knows what to think of it. First of all, Judah married a Canaanite woman. As a matter of fact, he moved away from his family and became very chummy with the Canaanites. It doesn't seem like he had regard for the godly Seed he was carrying, marrying a pagan woman. He had three sons. The first named Er, Judah married to Tamar. Er was so evil the Lord took his life. That must be pretty evil and not a real good testimony to Judah's life style. In those days a brother was supposed to raise up a child in his dead brother's name. Tamar was given to Judah's second son Onan. Onan did not cooperate. He refused to give Tamar his seed. Most likely he wanted the birthright of the firstborn. Because of this, he also died. Judah promised that when his third son was old enough, he would marry or provide his seed to Tamar. She was sent to live at her father's house. Now if all of the brothers refused her, Tamar was free to remarry. We aren't told all the details, but Judah never gave her his third son.

After Judah's wife died, Tamar dressed like a prostitute and sat at the side of the road. When Judah approached her for her services, she asked for his seal and cord as a surety for payment. Judah thought she was a temple prostitute. This was a pagan Canaanite ritual which would join him to the female fertility goddess of the Canaanites as an act of worship! How disrespectful is that! What little regard for the Seed!

Tamar became pregnant from this encounter with her father-in-law. When Judah found out Tamar was pregnant, he was going to have her burned. Tamar showed him the signet and cord. Judah repented and realized she was more righteous than he was.

Who had regard for the seed in this story? Certainly not Judah. He married a pagan woman. His sons were evil. And then he was willing to "give" his seed (holy, set apart seed) to a false goddess.

Tamar, on the other hand was fighting for the seed. She regarded it more than her own life. I know we generally look at this as a horrible sin, but remember in this culture it was the duty of the family to raise up a child in the brother's name. If the brothers were unable, the duty would go to the next of kin. Tamar was contending for her right to "the Seed" the covenant seed of Abraham and his household. Look at the odds of her getting pregnant from a single encounter. I believe Tamar's faith pulled "The Seed" to the line of Judah.

When Tamar's twins were born, we have another strange coincidence. The first child Zerah put his hand out. The midwife tied a scarlet cord on his hand to designate him as the firstborn. Then the second child, Perez, was born first. Even though the struggle was not as dramatic as with Jacob and Esau, we have the struggle between the brothers and the firstborn coming second.

Another strange coincidence: we have a similar situation as when Jacob adopted Joseph's two sons and blessed the younger over the older. Jacob could have been considered both Ephraim and Manasseh's father and grandfather. Judah when he fathered Perez and Zerah was raising up a seed for his son, and yet they were his sons. He was both their father and their grandfather. Ephraim received the birthright from Jacob. Perez received the kingly line and "The Seed" from Judah. Why? It seems to me that Tamar was the reason. From Judah's own mouth, she was more righteous than he. Tamar is mentioned in the book of Ruth as a blessing.

"Moreover, may your house be like the house of Perez whom Tamar bore to Judah..." Ruth 4:12

Tamar is also mentioned in the genealogy of Jesus. She seems to be honored, not dishonored. Here is something else to consider. The name Tamar means palm tree. In Solomon and Ezekiel's temple the walls were carved alternately with palm trees and cherubim. The cherubim had the face of a lion and a man. Could the cherubim represent Messiah as prophesied in Jacob's blessing over Judah (he was the Lion of the Tribe of Judah and a man) and the palm tree represent Tamar? I don't know. It is a possibility.

Rahab and Ruth

Two foreign women, Rahab and Ruth by faith joined themselves to Israel and became carriers of "The Seed". Rahab was a prostitute who lived in the wall of Jericho at the time when Joshua and all Israel marched around the city. Rahab had protected Joshua's two spies and helped them escape. The spies told her if she left a scarlet cord in the window everyone inside of her house would be saved. Her faith not only saved her household, but she became part of the line of Christ and carried the seed.

Ruth was a Moabite who had married an Israelite. When her father-in-law, brother-in--law and husband all died, she followed her mother-in-law back to Israel. She spoke these beautiful words to Naomi her mother-in-law.

Ruth 1:16-18 *"Do not urge me to leave you or turn back from following you; for where you go, I will go, and where you lodge, I will lodge. Your people shall be my people and your God, my God. Where you die, I will die and there I will be buried. Thus, may the Lord do to me, and worse if anything but death parts you and me."*

Her story is a beautiful type of Jesus as the kinsman redeemer. A kinsman redeemer is a close relative who can pay back a debt, avenge a wrong or restore the rights of a close family member. We will talk about Ruth a little later in the book.

Ruth's faith brought her into the covenant nation of Israel and into the line of Christ. I am reminded again of the quote I made earlier, by brother Kenneth Hagin, "Faith will cause God to bypass everyone and get to you"

Surely, in the journey of "The Seed", the birth order, birthright, and even the blessing give way to faith.

Chapter 9

Jesus The Man

Did you ever have a Bible verse that just kind of bugs you? It doesn't make sense, and you just kind of want to rewrite it for God. Well, I have had a few of those. Three, actually, that I can think of right now. All three of them have turned into beautiful revelations, that I just didn't understand at first. Imagine that! God was right all along. I was just ignorant. One of those verses was Hebrews 1:5 *"For to which of the angels did He ever say 'You are My Son, today I have begotten You?' And again, I will be a Father to Him and He shall be a Son to Me?"*

What really brought this to my attention, years ago, was we knew some really wonderful believers who got off into some wrong doctrine. They didn't believe Jesus was the Son of God (even though it is clear in John 1:1), but that he became the son of God. They used this scripture to validate a wrong teaching. I really couldn't understand it. Both how Christians could get off like that, and why this scripture is worded this way. How could there be a day when God said, *"Today I have begotten you."*? Jesus was eternally with the Father. There was no beginning to their relationship. It was eternal. Why *"Today, I have begotten you."*? This did not make sense to me at all.

After doing some cross referencing I found out when God said this. He said it when He raised Jesus from the dead. In Acts 13:33 it says *"That God has fulfilled this promise to our children in that He raised up Jesus, as it is also written in the second Psalm 'You are My Son; today I have begotten you."* Okay, now we need to look in Psalm two. I love this. The Bible is giving us another clue. It makes me feel like a detective! If we look at Psalm 2:7-9 we get a peek into what God the Father said to Jesus at the resurrection. Psalm 2:7-9 *"I will surely tell of the*

131

decree of the Lord, He said to Me, 'You are My Son, Today I have begotten You. Ask of Me and I will give the nations as Your inheritance, and the very ends of the earth as Your possession. You shall break them with a rod of iron. You shall shatter them like earthenware."

Wow, so with what we learned in the book of Acts, we know we are seeing what transpired between God and Jesus, when Jesus rose from the dead! The word *decree* from this verse is a legal word. It is a *statue, allotment, a fixed order*. This verse is God's legal declaration over Jesus. Jesus the second person of the God-head laid aside His position, His authority as God, His divine power, and became a man. Then as man He became sin and on the cross overcame sin, through the power of His humility and obedience AS A MAN. If He had done it as God, it would have been of no value to us. It would not change our identity. But God said this to Jesus, the Man.

This book came from my pondering of these verses. You see, none of this makes sense until we really come to grips with the fact that Jesus actually became a man. Hopefully in the previous chapters, we established that Jesus was able to become a human being through Abraham, specifically through Abraham's faith. Jesus came to earth as Abraham's seed...as a man.

When I looked this up in my book of doctrines, it seems that the doctrinal stance on this topic is: Jesus was fully God and fully man. However, no one seems to be able to explain what that means. I am going to attempt to explain what I believe this means. And, yes, I am treading softly because I am on holy ground.

Philippians 2:5-8 *" Have this attitude* (from a few verses up, the attitude of humility of mind and regarding one another as more important than yourself*)...Have this attitude in yourselves which was also in Christ Jesus, who, although He existed in the form of God* (the word *form* in this verse is '*morphe*' meaning: the outward form being in harmony with the inner essence - so Jesus was God in form and essence) *did not regard equality with*

God a thing to be grasped (clung to, retained) *but emptied Himself* (The word *empty* means deprive of content, make unreal. What did Jesus empty himself of? His deity.) *taking the form of a bondservant, being made in the likeness of men. Being found in appearance as a man, He humbled Himself by becoming obedient to the point of death, even death on a cross."*

Here we see Jesus is God in both essence and form. But he didn't cling to His deity. He laid it aside, humbling Himself enough to become human. He was now the essence of God, (or had His nature) but not His form. He didn't stop there, he humbled Himself even further to die, and not just any death, a cursed death, a humiliating, horrifying death.

Aleph Tau

Remember when we talked about the Hebrew alphabet being pictograms and each letter having a meaning. Let's revisit that for a minute. We mentioned earlier how Jesus said *"I am the alpha and omega..."*, the first and last letter of the Greek alphabet. In Hebrew the first and last letter of the alphabet is the aleph and the tau. As we discussed before the aleph is an ox head. It stands for the strongest, or greatest which is ultimately God. The tau is a T or a cross. It means a sign, marker or covenant. The word aleph tau or *et* means a sign. It is often an untranslated word that marks the direct object in a sentence. It is in the first sentence of the bible. In the beginning created God...aleph tau.... the heavens and the earth. That aleph tau is the story of the gospel. The strongest and highest God (aleph) made a covenant on a (tau) cross. The crucifixion is literally on a Tau, a cross. Crucifixion wasn't performed until centuries later, but there it is: the highest made the lowest, the lamb slain from the foundation of the world. It is hidden right there in the first book, even the first sentence, of the Bible.

This message is also repeated in Isaiah 7:14 *"Therefore the Lord Himself will give you a **sign**: Behold a virgin will be with child and bear a son and she will call His name Immanuel."* The word for sign is the same word only another letter has been added. The *vav*. The *vav* is a picture of a nail. The word for sign is *aleph vav tau*. The strongest, highest nailed to a cross. The gospel is right there in the word *sign*! I love how God thinks! I love finding these special messages, hidden throughout the Bible. Jesus! He is All in all. He is the secret of the universe. He is the mystery of the ages. Everything points to Him! Really the passage in Philippians is right there in the word sign. The greatest emptied Himself and was nailed to a cross! The Lord is saying, I will, Myself, give you a sign, God nailed to a cross, behold a virgin will be with child......

It Had to be a Man

Hebrews chapter two talks about Jesus becoming a man. Verse seventeen says *"Therefore He had to be made like His brethren in all things, so that He might become a merciful and faithful high priest in things pertaining to God, to make propitiation for the sins of the people."*

Jesus, wasn't here for Himself. He was here to make propitiation for the sins of the people. A man, Adam carried the whole human race in his loins and brought us into sin and death. We couldn't be redeemed by God. It had to be a man. A man had to redeem us, but there was no man who could. *"And He saw that there was no man, and was astonished that there was no one to intercede. Then His own arm brought salvation to Him, and His righteousness upheld Him."* (Isaiah 59:16)

Looking back at Hebrews chapter two we see this theme throughout the chapter, Hebrews 2:9-11. *"But we do see Him who was made for a little while lower than the angels, namely Jesus, because of the suffering of death* crowned with glory and honor...., so that by the grace of God, He might taste death for everyone. For it was fitting for Him, for whom are all things and through whom are all things in bringing many sons to glory, to perfect the author of their salvation through suffering. For both He who sanctifies and those who are sanctified are all from one **Father,** for which reason He is not ashamed to call them brethren." In that last sentence, "For both He who sanctifies and those who are sanctified are all from one **Father."** The word father is not there. The Bible says that we and Jesus are from one. One what? The translators assume the word Father, but I feel this isn't totally accurate. We are from one flesh or creation. We are the same species.

What is the difference? The difference is: Jesus didn't call us brethren because we deserved it. When Adam fell, we were no longer from one Father. We were separated from the Father. No. Jesus was not ashamed to call us brethren because He lowered Himself and became one of us. If the word father would be used there, it would have to refer to Abraham, not God. Abraham was the father of the Jewish people and the father of the "faith child", Jesus.

For that reason, "He is not **ashamed** to call us brethren." The word for ashamed epaisxymonai is ripe with meaning. It means bringing on fitting shame that matches the error of wrongly identifying or aligning with something. Jesus is not shaming Himself or wrongly identifying Himself with us as brethren. We are of the same family, race, DNA.

So, was Jesus fully God and fully man? Of course, that all depends on what that means. He was still Himself. He still had His divine nature, His essence, His person, but He laid aside His deity. He was not omniscient, omnipotent or omnipresent.

I remember when I was in high school, I saw a movie about Noah's Ark at the theater. The movie portrayed legends about Jesus as a boy traveling to other lands and doing miracles. It kind of gave me the creeps, but at the time I didn't have the knowledge to know why. Now I know, Jesus was a man. He never performed miracles until He was anointed by the Holy Spirit when John the Baptist baptized Him. When Jesus turned water into wine, the gospel of John says *"This was the beginning of signs Jesus did in Cana of Galilee and manifested His glory* and *His disciples believed on Him."* Jesus did miracles as a **man** filled with the Holy Spirit. Acts 10:38 *"You know how God **anointed** Jesus of Nazareth with the Holy Spirit and power and how He went about doing good and healing all who were oppressed by the devil **for God was with Him**."* Let's examine this verse a little bit. God anointed Jesus with the Holy Spirit and power. Jesus the eternal Word, the creator of the universe, didn't need to be anointed and given power. Jesus the **Man** did! Jesus the man needed the Holy Spirit to do the works of God.

The word *anointed* literally means *to smear or rub oil on something*, but to the Hebrew it meant God's Spirit coming on someone for a purpose. The kings, priests, and prophets were anointed for their tasks.

Jesus in His first sermon proclaimed that He was anointed for a purpose. He quoted the scripture about Himself that is in Isaiah 61.

"And the book of the prophet Isaiah was handed to Him. And He opened the book and found the place where it was written, 'The Spirit of the Lord is upon Me, because He anointed Me to preach the gospel to the poor. He has sent Me to proclaim release to the captives, and recovery of sight to the blind, to set free those who are oppressed, to proclaim the favorable year of the Lord.'" Luke 4:17-18 Jesus was heralding a new time, when we can come to God freely. But He was anointed by the Holy Spirit to do so. He did it as a man. He did it as Abraham's seed. He did miracles as a man led by the Holy Spirit.

Jesus himself said *"but the father abiding in me does His works."*

Jesus was a man. Jesus was a man! It blows me away. He didn't come to show us what God on earth looks like. He came to show us what man anointed by the Holy Spirit submitted to God looks like. I think we have spiritualized everything He did so much, that we haven't let it really sink in. He didn't come as God. He came as a man. He came as the seed of woman and as the seed of Abraham. He wasn't showing us what God should look like. (That isn't totally true, He was representing God's nature. But that is what we should do too!) He was showing us what **we** should look like.

Irenaeus and the Temptation of Jesus

A few years back I found a free book on the internet. It was mailed to me with no strings attached. It is called *The Antichrist.* The book is a reprint of some of the writings of two early church fathers, Irenaeus and Hippolytus. I found Irenaeus' writing particularly fascinating. He discusses the temptation of Jesus in the wilderness and brings out some points that I never realized before. After Jesus had fasted for forty days and was hungry, Satan appeared to Him and said, *"If you are the Son of God, command that these stones become bread."* (Matthew 4:3)

Jesus answered and said, *"It is written, 'Man shall not live on bread alone, but on every word that proceeds out of the mouth of God.'"* (Matthew 4:4)

We get our attention on the bread, and don't fully see what is happening here. Satan said, "**If you are the Son of God...**" Jesus answered, "**Man** *shall not live by bread alone...*" Jesus didn't even address if He was the Son of God! He identified Himself as **man** and therefore under the law!

Here is what Irenaeus says. **"As to those words [of His enemy], "If thou be the Son of God," [the Lord]** made no remark; but by thus acknowledging His human nature He baffled His adversary, and exhausted the force of his first attack by means of His Father's word. The corruption of man therefore, which occurred in paradise by both [of our first parents] eating, was done away with by [the Lord's] want of food in this world ..."[28] After discussing the second temptation Irenaeus says, **"The pride of reason, therefore, which was in the serpent, was put to naught by the humility found in the man [Christ], and now twice was the devil conquered from Scripture..."[29]** I love that! The pride of reason, was destroyed by the humility of THE MAN, JESUS CHRIST! Jesus in humility and total subjection to the Word of God, defeated Satan. Can I reiterate this? A Man totally subjected Himself to the written Word of God and in obedience and humility confounded and bound Satan's authority!

Irenaeus expounds on this idea. He makes some amazing assertions. Some of them, I really don't feel knowledgeable enough to make a definitive statement, and yet they are so fascinating I want to share them with you.

Irenaeus says of Satan, **"For as in the beginning he enticed man to transgress his Maker's law, and thereby got him into his power, yet his power consists in transgression and apostasy, and with these he bound man [to himself]; so again, on the other hand, it was necessary that through man himself he should, when conquered, be bound with the same chains with which he had bound man, in order that man, being set free, might return to his Lord, leaving to him (Satan) those bonds which he himself had been fettered, that is, sin. For when Satan is bound, man is set free; since '_none can_**

---

[28] Larry Harper, _The Antichrist_, (The Elijah Project, Mesquite, TX,1992) p.11
[29] Ibid.

enter a strong man's house and spoil his goods, unless he first binds the strong man himself.' *(Matthew 12:29, Mark 3:27)* The Lord therefore exposes him as speaking contrary to the word of that God who made all things, and subdues him by means of the commandment. Now the law is the commandment of God. **The Man** proves him to be a fugitive from and a transgressor of the law, an apostate also from God. After [**the Man** had done this], the Word bound him securely as a fugitive from Himself, and made a spoil of his goods, namely those men whom he held in bondage..."[30]

Wow! He is saying is that...Satan trapped and bound man with the cords of sin and apostasy. We were enslaved to Satan by the power of sin. And yet **The Man** Jesus Christ came. He was not controlled by sin. He was humble and obedient! He through His obedience proved Satan's guilt and rebellion against the Law! He bound Satan with his own chains! Jesus was then able to plunder his house.

This is the first encounter between Jesus and Satan that we see in the framework of this earth. But this is not their first encounter. Not at all. Somewhere in the ages past Jesus created Lucifer. He was a servant of the Almighty God. They knew each other. Lucifer once knew the heart of God. He once worshipped Him, but Lucifer's heart became full of pride and he traded the glory of knowing God for the lust to be god. He desired to be exalted above Him. He found out that he was no contest for the Mighty One. Satan contented himself with repulsing God with the depravity he could bring to God's creation. He enslaved mankind to sin. And now here it seemed like God's weak-minded love for mankind had served his dream to him on a silver platter. Here before him was God, hardly recognizable. This half-starved, filthy wilderness weakened son of Abraham was the Lord of

---

[30] Ibid.pp.12-13

Creation! The Mighty One! The Master would finally get a taste of servanthood. And he, Satan, would put his foot on His neck, so to speak, and rub His face in Satan's supremacy. The eternal God was in his territory now!

Yet, Jesus the Man in all his physical weakness would not do what Lucifer (and Adam) did in all their glory. He would not exalt Himself. He would not question God. He would not disobey the Word of God!

There is a song that calls Jesus "a rose trampled on the ground..." I think of the incense of myrrh. In its crushing, a fragrant aroma is released. This was not the ultimate crushing of Messiah, when not only His physical body, but his spirit and soul would be put to the ultimate test. That would come 3 years later. This physical crushing of Jesus, the Man, produced a fragrant aroma. They say when you're squeezed what is in you comes out. If you are an orange you will get orange juice. If you are a lemon, you will get lemon juice. If you are full of anger and bitterness, that will come out under pressure. When Jesus was squeezed, when He was crushed, we see no self-will, only submission, obedience, and faith. We see the Beauty of Holiness!

According to Irenaeus, when Jesus the Man submitted to the law and spoke it forth, He bound Satan under sin. Perhaps this encounter was necessary for Jesus ministry. It certainly happened in the beginning of His ministry, before He had done any miracles. Perhaps this was the binding of the strongman so He could plunder his house. I already quoted this verse but it bears repeating, *"For it was fitting for Him, for whom are all things, and through whom are all things, in bringing many sons to glory, to perfect the author of their salvation through sufferings. For both He who sanctifies* (Jesus) *and those who are sanctified* (us) *are all from one* (we are the same creation, He was a man) *for which reason He is not ashamed* (He is not wrongfully identifying us) *to call us brethren..."* Jesus had to be one of us, to redeem us.

He is Still a Man

And that is not the only shocker.... He is still a man! That totally blows me away. I remember the first time I ever heard this. It was 37 years ago. I was sitting in a Bible class. I was shocked then. I still am today. Jesus is a born-again man. He will never go back to being what He was before the incarnation. He will always be a born-again man. Please don't freak out, I am not saying He isn't God, because of course He is. But the power and authority He gained back, He gained back as a man. He brought us along with Him.

Just in case you think I am totally crazy, and I wouldn't blame you, because I still can't wrap my head around this, I am going to quote to you out of a respected book of doctrine. This is from *Outline Studies in Christian Doctrine* by George Pardington Ph. D. This doctrine is called "perpetuity".

"It is the unmistakable teaching of the Scriptures that the Son of God assumed forever the humanity which He assumed at His birth by the virgin. The incarnation is in perpetuity. For this there are principally three reasons

1. **It is essential to the integrity of our Lord's manhood....**
2. **It is essential to our Lord's high priestly intercession...**
3. **It is essential to our Lord's return and millennial reign..."[31]**

What Jesus did for us, what He was willing to go through, what He was able to accomplish is HUGE! It is weighty. I think it is actually inconceivable. Everything

---

[31] George P. Pardington, Ph.D. *Outline Studies in Christian Doctrine,* Harrisburg, Penn., Christian Publications Inc. 1926) pp. 230-231

Jesus obtained as a man, He already had as God. He already was higher than any other creation. He laid everything aside and gained it all back again as man! It was for our benefit. Jesus the eternal co-creator with the Father, the one who holds this time-space continuum with the Word of His Power, emptied Himself. He confined eternity to time. He confined omniscience to a human brain. He confined His omnipresence to a human body and His omnipotence to faith in God. He lived a life of total obedience and dependence on the Father. Everything He accomplished, He accomplished **as** a man, so that He could accomplish it **for** man.

He Learned Obedience Through the Things He Suffered

Quite a few years ago, I was complaining to God while I was washing my dishes. I was mad at my husband and saying something like "Jesus, you don't know what this is like. You just had to obey God and He is perfect. I am here with a control freak. You never had to deal with that. You didn't have to do things hard and unreasonable!" (I was mad.)

I heard the Lord answer me. "Nah uh uh uh!" (Really that's what He said.)

All of these scenes from Jesus life began to go through my mind. I began to see His life, like I had never seen it before, and I knew it was all in obedience to the Father.

I saw Jesus as a boy at age twelve. He was passionate for the things of the Father and stayed at the temple. But in obedience, he went back home and submitted to His parents. I saw Jesus first sermon, in His own home town. It was before friends, relatives, friends of His parents, people He had known His whole life. I realized Jesus, like everyone else wanted to do well and have people appreciate what He said. I remember my first public message. I felt so vulnerable. I really wanted some positive feedback. Jesus **was** getting positive feedback! At first, they were in awe of His wisdom, except He kept talking!   By the time He was done, they were trying to throw Him off a cliff! Nice feedback to your first sermon, among your own folks!

Why didn't He just stop talking while everyone was still happy and marveling at His words? Obedience to the Father.

When He healed the man with a withered arm, why did He do it on the Sabbath? Why couldn't He just wait a day? Then no one could have gotten upset. Why not heal on Sunday or Monday? Obedience to the Father.

In John chapter six, Jesus had a huge following. Everyone was excited to hear Him. He had miraculously fed the multitude and had quite a momentum going. Then He talked about eating His body and drinking His blood? What is that supposed to mean? Cannibalism? It certainly wasn't something a nice Jewish man would say. The crowds left Him. Why didn't Jesus say it a little differently, or why say it at all? Obedience to the Father.

When I looked at Jesus' life, I realized it was hard! He lived a hard life! God never really allowed Him to have the approval of others. He was constantly misunderstood. He was slandered. He was always saying and doing things that made people mad.

Standing there doing my dishes, I saw Jesus life. A life of obedience, but not a life of ease or pleasure. And I saw His heart. I actually saw that it looked like a pure diamond, a perfect diamond. There was no self-will, no pride, no selfish ambition, nothing held back for Himself. It was totally submitted to the Father. It was a perfect heart. I thought of the verse when Jesus said, "*The ruler of this world is coming and he has nothing in Me.*"

There was nothing Satan, the accuser, could point to, accuse or get a hold of Jesus by. His heart was one of total obedience and total submission. Hebrews 5:8 says "*although He was a Son, He learned obedience through the things He suffered.*"

Everything in Jesus' life was preparing Him for that final act of obedience. God wasn't being mean to Him. He was teaching Him never to rely on the praise of men. Like Paul said, *"If I was still trying to please men, I would not be the bond-servant of God.".* (Gal.1:10)

Jesus obedience, affection, approval, and identity were the Father. He had to learn to forgive unfair treatment and walk in the Father's love. Remember earlier in the book we talked about the spirit realm. In the spirit realm it is what is in your heart that matters, not just how you act. The Pharisees could look holy and flaunt their righteousness, but even though they didn't commit adultery or murder or theft outwardly, in their hearts that is what they were. If Jesus, on the cross, had said *"Forgive them Father"* but inwardly was raging with anger or unforgiveness or self-pity, it wouldn't have been good enough. He had to forgive from the heart. He learned that through a lifetime of obedience and surrender.

Hebrews 5:7 *"In the days of His flesh, He offered up both prayers and supplications with loud crying and tears to the One able to save Him from death, and He was heard because of His piety (*Piety is *eulabeias and means reverent submission). Although He was a Son, He learned obedience from the things which He suffered, and having been made **perfect**, He became to all those who obey Him the source of eternal salvation.*

That word *perfect*, in Greek *"elio"*, means I complete or accomplish, made perfect as a course, race, I complete, finish. It is the same word used in Hebrews 2:10 *"It was fitting for Him ...to **perfect** the author of their salvation through sufferings."*

There is a song that says "I'll never know how much it cost, to see my sin upon that cross." I believe that is true. Can we really understand what He did for us? What He did for **man** as **man**. I believe we have religiously brushed off Jesus as being God, therefore it was easy for Him. No! He was a man. When He went to hell, He didn't pull out the God card. He didn't overcome as God. He

144

overcame as a man. Look at this verse, "*In the days of His flesh, He offered up both prayers and supplications with loud crying and tears to the One able **to save Him from death,** and He was heard **because of His piety.**"* He was heard because of His piety or reverent submission, not because He was God, but because as a man He was obedient.

Hebrews 7:16 talks about Jesus becoming a high priest according to the order of Melchizedek. If you confer Ps. 2, Ps. 110 and Acts 13:33 you will see this happened at Christ's resurrection. Hebrews 7:16 says Jesus became a high priest according to the order of Melchizedek by the **power of an indestructible life.** That word indestructible means not able to be abolished, destroyed or overthrown. Jesus' life and obedience were how He overcame death as a man for men.

I heard an amazing testimony on the *"It's Supernatural"* T.V. show with Sid Roth. A man named Kevin Zadai died during a dental procedure and had an encounter with Jesus. The story can be read in his book "*Heavenly Visitation"*. While Kevin talked with Jesus, Jesus told him how He meditated on scripture about Himself, in particular Psalm 16. When Jesus was in hell, He could no longer feel the Father and the Holy Spirit. He was abandoned. He stood in faith on the verse, "*For you will not abandon my soul to Sheol. Neither will You allow Your Holy One to undergo decay.*" He knew the Father would raise Him up. He meditated on the scripture in faith, just as we humans need to do today. We need to find out who we are in scripture and stand in faith on His promises.

At the beginning of this chapter I talked about the verse that started this whole thought process in me. Hebrews 1:5 "*For to which of the angels did He ever say 'You are My Son; Today I have begotten You.*" Jesus always lived with the Father. "*In the beginning was the Word, and the Word was with God, and the Word was God.*" John 1:1. Jesus was intrinsically God and was part of the Godhead. He laid His deity aside. He laid aside His equality with God. He was born of a woman. (He was not born of a man. Therefore, He did not inherit the generational curse of spiritual death passed down through Adam and every father since.) He lived a perfect life. A life totally submitted to the Word of God. He fulfilled the Law. He was the perfect man. He was the intercessor.

Then the Bible says something pretty outrageous. That *"He made Him who knew no sin **to be** sin on our behalf, so that we might become the righteousness of God in Him."* Romans 5:21 That perfect God-Man was made to BE sin! As sin, He was forsaken of God! He had no standing.

Isaiah 53:10 says *"But the Lord was pleased to crush Him putting Him to grief; If He would render Himself as a guilt offering."* Literally in Hebrew it says "*When thou shall make His soul guilt*".

When I was in Bible school, we learned about a type of Christ that was at first troubling to me. It was the brazen serpent in the wilderness.

Numbers 21:4-9 *"Then they set out from Mount Hor by the way of the Red Sea, to go around the land of Edom. And the people became impatient because of the journey. The people spoke against God and Moses, 'Why have you brought us up out of Egypt to die in the wilderness? For there is no food and no water, and we loathe this miserable food.' The Lord sent fiery serpents among the people and they bit the people so that many people of Israel died. So, the people came to Moses and said, 'We have sinned, because we have spoken against the Lord and you; intercede with the Lord that He may remove the serpents from us.' And Moses interceded for the people. Then the Lord said to Moses, 'Make a fiery serpent and set it on a standard: and it shall come about that everyone who is bitten, when he looks at it, he shall live.' And Moses made a bronze serpent and set it on the standard; and it came about, that if a serpent bit any man, when he looked to the bronze serpent, he lived."*

This is one of the few types of Christ that Jesus himself makes reference to. In John 3:14 Jesus said, *"As Moses lifted up the serpent in the wilderness, even so must the Son of Man be lifted up."*

The serpent as a type of Christ! That is what made me uncomfortable. Everyone knows a serpent is a symbol of evil. That bothered me! A serpent should not represent Jesus. Then I learned that the brazen serpent represents Christ on the cross **as our sin**! Brass represents judgement. The picture is God's judgement on Christ as our sin on the cross. As we look to Christ the Man bearing our guilt and judgement, we are healed!

So, this is why, God had a specific time, at the resurrection of Christ when He said *"Thou art My Son, today I have begotten Thee."* He said this to Jesus, The Man, risen from the dead, having conquered death, hell and the grave! Jesus laid aside all claim to sonship as God. He was then a damned soul, who became sin. Then because of His perfect submission and perfect blood, the price was paid. God said *"Thou art my son, today I have begotten Thee."* to Jesus the Man, head and progenitor of the new race of mankind!

Chapter 10

Jesus the Seed

In the same way that Adam was the progenitor of the human race, Jesus is the progenitor of the race of born-again sons of God. Adam carried the physical seed of every human being within himself. Jesus carries the spiritual seed of every born-again son of God!

Jesus was a seed. He was the seed of Abraham, but He was also a heavenly seed. He was seed planted by God to propagate sons in the earth. Jesus was planted in the ground in death. His death produced a harvest. For not only did He rise to new life, He began a brand-new race. He multiplies Himself in all of those who believe in Him.

Hebrew 12:2 *"fixing our eyes on Jesus, the **author** and **perfecter** of faith, who for the joy set before Him endured the cross, despising the shame, and has sat down at the right hand of the throne of God"*

The word for *author* there is *archegos*, which means *the first in a long procession, a file leader who pioneers the way for many others to follow.*

The word perfecter is *teleiotes* meaning *consummator, bringing the process to a finish.*

We could say: *"Fixing our eyes on Jesus the pioneer, originator and consummator of faith, who for the joy set before Him endured the cross..."*

What was the joy set before Him?

Why did He endure the cross?

We are! We are why He endured the cross. He was looking to us, the new creation.

In John 12:24 Jesus says about His death, *"Truly, truly, I say to you, unless a grain of wheat falls into the earth and dies, it remains alone, but if it dies, it bears much fruit."*

149

Jesus was the grain of wheat. He was going to die.
He was being planted to bear fruit.

We are the fruit Jesus bore. How does seed
reproduce?

After its own kind!!!! When we are born again, we
are born of His seed. We are the plant that grows from
him being buried in the ground. **We are His kind**.

The Feast of First Fruits

Many years ago, after doing much research, I was
appalled to find out all of our holidays are pagan (except
Thanksgiving)! They are pagan holidays with a Christian
veneer. My plan was going to be to throw out all those
pagan holidays and celebrate the Feasts of Israel. The
Jewish feasts are jam packed with truth. They illustrate,
illuminate and foretell God's plan of redemption.

It's now many years later and regrettably the only
Jewish festival I have successfully worked into our family
traditions is Passover. This is the easiest one, because
we celebrate it along with Resurrection Sunday in lieu of
Easter. I realized something along the way. Even though
we celebrate the holidays with our family, we celebrate
them as a culture or as a community. I mean, many years
I have totally forgotten Pentecost, Trumpets and the other
Jewish festivals. (Besides the fact that I couldn't figure
out just how to celebrate them. It was more of a
community celebration.) But could you imagine forgetting
Christmas? Impossible…it is right in your face. As you
have probably noticed, retail stores start putting out
Christmas stock at the end of August! Whether we
celebrate them or not, the Jewish festivals are our
heritage. They also predict future events. We do need to
study them. They are primary to an understanding of the
past and future events of prophecy.

There are seven festivals in all. Because it is such a
large topic, I will be brief. The first three are in the spring.
They run together and overlap. The Feast of Unleavened

Bread, Passover, and First Fruits. These three have already been fulfilled with Jesus' first coming. The Feast of Unleavened Bread represents Jesus holy life. He died on Passover and He rose again on First Fruits. Everything that Jesus represented in these three feasts, happened at the exact time the Jews were "rehearsing" them. Jesus' last week on earth followed exactly what happened to the Passover lambs. Even as the lamb was being slaughtered, Jesus was crucified. But another lesser known feast, The Feast of First Fruits, also coincides with these events.

This feast commemorated the beginning of the grain harvest. A special sheaf of barley was being marked for the offering. The harvest was not to be touched until that first sheaf of barley was offered and waved before the Lord. This represents Jesus, the first fruits of the New Birth and the resurrection from the dead! At the time the Jewish officials were marking the barley to be offered, Jesus was standing before the high priest Caiaphas.

Caiaphas had prophesied earlier *"You know nothing at all, nor do you take into account that it is expedient for you that one man die for the people, and that the whole nation not perish."*

He was marking Jesus not only as the Passover lamb, but as the barley sheaf. While they were binding the sheaf for the offering, Jesus was being bound and led away to be crucified. Then on the Sunday after the Passover, the sheaf was to be waved before the Lord. This is when Jesus was resurrected. Once that barley sheaf was offered, the rest of the barley was sanctified and ready to be harvested. Jesus was our first fruits offering that made the rest of us holy. He was resurrected and the first born from the dead. We will also be resurrected when the harvest is complete.

"But now Christ has been raised from the dead, the **first fruits** *of those who are asleep."* 1 Corinthians 15:20

*"For those whom He foreknew, He also predestined to become conformed to the image of His Son, so that He would be the **firstborn among many brothers.**" Romans 8:29*

When we are born again, the seed that produces our new life also produces the nature of Christ in us! Or as this verse says we are to be conformed to the image of Jesus.

The Crazy Horse Memorial

Years ago, my daughter was moving from the West Coast back to Michigan. I flew to her house and spent a few days with her. Then we packed up her car and headed East. Because neither one of us had ever been through that part of the country before, we decided to take it slow and see some sights along the way. What really excited me was that we were going to visit Mount Rushmore. I had always wanted to go there. Since I was a kid, I have seen pictures of it in history books, seen it depicted in movies, T.V. shows, and even cartoons. Now I was finally going to see it in person.   But we made a stop just before going to Mount Rushmore that so moved me, Mount Rushmore was actually anti-climactic. That stop we made was to Crazy Horse Memorial.

Crazy Horse Memorial is an unfinished carving of the Native American hero, Crazy Horse. It is being sculpted on the side of Thunderhead Mountain. When it is finished it will be the largest statue in the world. Driving up to the memorial complex, you can see the huge face jutting out from the mountain. My first reaction was awe. You just can't help being amazed at something of that scale. My second reaction was disappointment. I felt impatient. I wanted it to be completed, so I could be amazed at the whole statue.

My daughter and I parked and went inside a large museum. We really didn't know what to expect, but we found a theater inside the museum. We went in and watched the story of the monument and the sculptor. It was this story that so deeply moved me.

The vision for Crazy Horse Memorial began with Henry Standing Bear, an Oglala Lakota chief and relative of Crazy Horse. Standing Bear wanted a Native American hero to be honored along with the Presidents on Mount Rushmore. It seemed unfitting to ignore the Native American on land that was supposed to be deeded to the Native people forever. He wrote to the sculptor Gutzon Borglum, but never received an answer.

Meanwhile, Korczak Ziolkowski was a promising upcoming sculptor. One of his works won first prize in the World's Fair in 1939. This led to his being invited to work on Mount Rushmore with Gutzon Borglum. As Korczak's notoriety was beginning to grow, he responded to a letter from Henry Standing Bear asking him to carve a monument of Crazy Horse, to honor the Native Americans. Korczak, was a bachelor sculptor in his late thirties. He moved to South Dakota and began what would become his life's work. He is quoted as saying, **"By carving Crazy Horse, if I can give back to the Indian some of his pride and create a means to keep alive his culture and heritage, my life will have been worthwhile."**[32]

The project was an incredible undertaking. On top of all that, Korczak and Standing Bear refused any government help. They did not trust the government's commitment to keep true to the goal of honoring Native Americans. After almost 36 years of work, Korczak died unexpectedly. At the time of his death, the monument was unrecognizable! Korczak's life work was unfinished with nothing really to show for it.

It seemed to me that, that might have been the end of the dream and the end of Crazy Horse Memorial. All the work and dreams of Standing Bear and Korczak

---

[32] "Meet Korczak-Storyteller in Stone" Crazy Horse Memorial, crazyhorsememorial.org (accessed Jan. 15, 2019)

Ziolkowski could have been for nothing, just empty wasted dreams.

Except…. except!!!

In 1950, Korczak married a lovely, young lady, Ruth Ross. Not only did Ruth share the vision and dream of Crazy Horse, so did their 10 children! Korczak build a schoolhouse on the property and not only were his children taught regular subjects, they learned how to carve mountains and carry on his work!

His dream was too big for one man, but he was a seed! He reproduced himself and his vision. The work goes on. His wife and children have carried on the vision. After his passing, his wife, Ruth, had the foresight to work primarily on the statue's face, which was completed in 1998. A wise move, for now the thousands of visitors can see the completed face and also catch the excitement of the project.

What a different outcome it could have been. Korczak went to South Dakota as one man to carve a statue out of a mountain. Yet, while he was there something even greater happened. He reproduced his vision in his family. A quote from the website states. **"The remarkable Ziolkowski Family is motivated by their individual and collective dedication, determination, and courage to carry on Korczak's work. They are supported by his great faith and confidence in them, schooled by his years of instruction, toughened by his example and uplifted by his sense of humor. They are also guided by his detailed plans and scale models and inspired by his life, vision, legacy, and most importantly, by what he often referred to as 'the beauty and justice of the Crazy Horse dream"[33]**

This is just my opinion, but I think Korczak's true greatness wasn't in his carving ability, it was in his fatherhood.

---

[33] The Ziolkowski Family" Crazy Horse Memorial, crazyhorsememorial.org (accessed Jan.15, 2019)

Just as Korczak Ziolkowski was able to reproduce his dream, skill and abilities into his family, his seed, we are Jesus seed. We are birthed by His faith, changed by His nature. We share His dreams. We continue what He started. We are an extension of who He is and what He is like. We are His offspring!

Jesus' Seed

The whole purpose of our Christian lives is to reproduce Jesus' nature. We take on His image and likeness. We are literally Jesus seed. It seems like a figurative kind of thing. But it is not. It is real in the spirit realm. The Bible actually mentions Jesus' seed, which is what the born-again Christian is.

Isaiah 53:10-11 *"But the Lord was pleased to crush Him, putting Him to grief; if He would render Himself as a guilt offering. **He will see His offspring**. He will prolong His days, and the good pleasure of the Lord will prosper in His hand. As a result of the anguish of His soul, **He will see and be satisfied**: By His knowledge the Righteous One, My servant will justify the many, and He will bear their iniquities."*

Verse ten says literally *"He will see His **seed**."* Couple that phrase with *"As a result of the anguish of His soul, He will see and be satisfied* (or have His desired fulfilled.)" What will He see and be satisfied? His seed.

So, we could paraphrase this verse: *"He will see His seed, as a result of the anguish of His soul, He will see His seed and have His desire fulfilled."*

This is the Old Testament counterpart to Hebrews 12:2 *"Who for the joy set before Him endured the cross..."*

Why was Jesus enduring? ... to see His seed... that is us. We are the joy set before Him. We are His desire fulfilled. We are His seed. He reproduces Himself in the born-again *believer*.

From Faith to Faith

I'd like to get into the "nuts and bolts" of this whole process. Can I just be a little real here for a minute? I expect you to check out the scriptures and make sure what I am saying is true. I believe it is true or I wouldn't be writing it. Of course, you can believe what I say or not, with or without my permission. I say all that, because what I am going to say next is "hot off the revelation press." I was lying in bed pondering these things and it hit me. I haven't had months or years to meditate on this one, but at the same time I feel it is important, so I am going to say it.

I have always thought the "soil" of the parable of the sower or the "egg" of the new birth was our hearts. The word enters our heart and we are born again. What even is our heart? Many times, we don't define these terms. I believe the heart of man is the combination of the soul (mind, will and emotions) and the spirit. So, it is that part of man that is not physical. The spirit is the inner essence of who you are. The soul seems to be the middle ground, that can either express the physical outward man or the inner spirit man.

The word of God goes into our heart, but there is something within our heart that it is united with, in order for conception or germination to take place. What is that something? Of course, it is hiding in plain sight. I don't know why I didn't see it before. The word doesn't germinate directly, there is something within our heart, just like the egg is in the womb.

It is our faith!

The word of faith meets faith in the heart and bam! New birth takes place. Like meets like. This also illuminates one of those verses that just didn't make sense to me.

Romans 1:16-17 *"For I am not ashamed of the gospel, for it is the power* (dynamite power) *of God for salvation to everyone who believes, to the Jew first and also to the Greek, for in it* (the gospel) *the righteousness of God is revealed from* **faith to faith***; as it is written, 'But the righteous man shall live by faith.'"*

I never quite got what the **faith to faith** was. Now I do. When God speaks, He speaks faith.

"But having the same spirit of faith, according to what is written, 'I believed therefore I spoke,' we also believe therefore we also speak," 2 Corinthians 4:13

This is how God speaks. He speaks out of faith and His words always produce.

"For My thoughts are not your thoughts, neither are your ways My ways, declares the Lord. For as the heavens are higher than the earth, so are My ways higher than your ways and My thoughts than your thoughts. For as the rain and the snow come down from heaven, and do not return there without watering the earth and making it bear and sprout, and furnishing seed to the sower and bread to the eater; so shall My word be which goes forth from My mouth; it shall not return to Me empty, without accomplishing what I desire, and without succeeding in the matter for which I sent it." Isaiah 54:8-11

Isn't that interesting? When God speaks His word, it goes forth and accomplishes what He sent it out to do. This is because His word is spoken in perfect faith. And then it returns to Him like the rain and snow return to the clouds.

This reminds me of Hebrews 1:1 and also John 1:14.

"God, after He spoke long ago to the fathers in the prophets in many portions and in many ways, **in these last days has spoken to us in His Son***..."*

*"**And the Word became flesh,** and dwelt among us, and we saw His glory, glory as of the only begotten from the Father, full of grace and truth."*

In these last days, the days of salvation, God has spoken His word to us, Jesus. Only He wasn't just a spoken word, He was a word that was manifested in our realm. He was a flesh and blood word. He was sent to the earth. Jesus watered the earth. He made it bear and sprout. He returned to the Father having accomplished what he intended. He made the earth...He made the spirit of man who is dust, bear and sprout!

What is the **faith to faith**? It is God's faith uniting with our faith! The gospel is God's faith. It enters the heart of man and is combined with our faith. BAM! An explosion takes place! A birth. The curse of sin is reversed and the spirit of man is united to the Spirit of God.

God's faith, Jesus' faith is the gospel. It is all that Jesus came and did. When this truth is heard and understood, it is the DNA of God. When it is combined with our faith it germinates and grows into the likeness and nature of Christ, thirty, sixty, and a hundredfold. In Hebrews chapters three and four, salvation is compared to the children of Israel entering the promised land.

*"For indeed we have had good news preached to us, just as they also; but the **word** they heard did not profit them, because it was not **united by faith** in those who heard. For we who have **believed** (have faith) enter that rest…"* Hebrew 4:2-3

What do the word and faith produce? Christ!

*"To whom God willed to make known what is the riches of the glory of this mystery among the Gentiles, **which is Christ in you the hope of glory**."* Col.1:27

Abraham and Mary

Abraham and Mary's miraculous births are types of the new birth. Abraham was promised a seed, Jesus, in whom all the nations of the earth would be blessed. But how can he have a seed if he has no child? God's promise united with Abraham's faith birthed Isaac. Isaac was a type or proxy of Christ. Isaac was a supernatural birth. Isaac carried the Promised Seed in his loins.

Abraham's faith in His seed, opened the door for Christ to come. Abraham was declared righteous. Christ in him was his hope of glory. The whole nation of Israel, in a sense, carried Christ. It was their faith in Messiah that made them a holy nation. It was Christ in them, their hope of glory.

Mary believed the word of Gabriel the angel. A word sent from the Father.

"The angel said to her, 'Do not be afraid, Mary, for you have found favor with God. And behold, you will conceive in your womb and bear a son, and you shall name Him Jesus. He will be great and will be called the Son of the Most High; and the Lord God will give Him the throne of His father David; and He will reign over the house of Jacob forever, and His kingdom will have no end ...And Mary said, 'behold the bond slave of the Lord; may it be done to me according to your word.' And the angel departed from her." Luke 1:30-33,38.

The word combined with her faith produced Christ in her. He, Christ, was her hope of glory. Abraham, the nation of Israel, and Mary carried the physical seed of Christ. They carried the promise that He would come in the flesh. When we hear the word, the gospel, the good news of what Jesus has done for us, and it is combined with faith in our hearts, the new birth takes place. We carry Jesus' nature in us. And it is His nature in us, Christ being formed in us, that is our hope of glory. We don't carry the physical Jesus in us like Abraham and Mary. But, just as real, a seed of heaven, of Jesus himself, has been planted in our hearts. We are no longer the seed of Adam. We carry the seed of the second Adam, Jesus. We are changing into His image, if we continue to walk in faith.

"For you have died (we died to being the old man, the old creation, the seed of Adam, we died to our fleshly self-centered nature) *and your life* (your born-again new life from Jesus' seed) *is hidden with Christ in God. When*

Christ who is our life is revealed, then you also will be revealed with Him in glory." Colossians 3:3-4

"Beloved, now we are children of God, and it has not appeared as yet what we will be. We know that when He appears, we will be like Him, because we will see Him just as He is." 1 John 3:2

Right now, we still look like Adam. We still have a body that is Adam's seed. But, hidden inside of us, something is growing and changing who we are! A new creation is being formed in us. One day we will get a new body that will show on the outside what we have become on the inside.

We Must Continue to Walk by Faith

It is just as important for us to continue our Christian life by faith. Many times, when we are first saved, we understand our righteousness is by faith in Christ alone, but somewhere along the line, we switch over to a works-based mentality. We start thinking things like, I have been a Christian for a long time now. God expects me to be able to perform. He expects more out of me. I should know better. I should do better than this.

*"Therefore, as you have received Christ Jesus the Lord, so walk in Him, having been **firmly rooted** and now being **built up** in Him and **established in your faith**, just as you were instructed and overflowing with gratitude."* Colossians 2:6-7

We received Jesus by faith, knowing that we were not capable of pleasing God with our own efforts. We continue to walk in Him in the same way. Let's look at some of the words in this verse.

"Firmly rooted" means planted, to take root. Sounds like the parable of the sower. Remember the seeds that didn't make it? They weren't firmly rooted.

"Built up" means to build on or above a foundation. Our seed grows up in faith. It continues to take on Christ nature by faith.

"Established" in the Greek this means to walk where it is solid. We live in an illusion. Don't we? Faith is where it is solid! I think of our outdated science from when I grew up. The science of that day screamed at us "if you can't see it, feel it or taste it, it is not real!" While they pounded their 99.9% empty space fist on their 99.9% empty space desk!

This verse is saying: trade in this physical, material, (empty space) realm for something solid, FAITH IN GOD! Now there is something solid. God. Depending on His faithfulness **is** walking on solid ground.   Walk where it is solid…on faith.

Our New Man, The Faith Man

Our "new man" is a faith man. This is why Paul reacted so strongly to the Galatians when they wanted to go back to practicing the Law. They were aborting the new birth. Let's look at a couple of the verses in Galatians, where Paul is rebuking the Galatians for trying to go back under the law!

"You foolish Galatians who has bewitched you, before whose eyes Jesus Christ was publicly portrayed as crucified? This is the only thing I want to find out from you: did you receive the Spirit by the works of the Law or by hearing with faith?"

"My children, with whom I am again in labor until Christ is formed in you…"

"You have been severed from Christ, you who are seeking to be justified by law; you have fallen from grace." Galatians 3:1-2, 4:19,5:4

Receive His Love

Those are some pretty strong words! If you, like I do, find yourself doubting God's love and forgiveness, if you feel you have to accomplish something on your own to deserve salvation, if you have to fit some sort of standard other than obedience to Jesus, let go of the law and step over into faith!

I have a personal illustration that I hope will help you. As I said earlier in the book, I have struggled with low self-esteem and insecurity. In the early days of my marriage, this really affected my relationship with my husband. I really didn't think that I deserved him, and I was afraid that sooner or later, he would figure that out. I was always trying to get him to do something to make me **feel** loved. I had this idea, although I never told him about it, that as long as I did more nice things for him, than he did for me, he would still love me.

As a young couple, we were pretty broke. We lived in our home town in Michigan at the time of this incident, but my mom and twin sister and their families lived in Florida. I was terribly homesick for them and had not seen them in several years. This was in the days before unlimited long-distance phone calls. My sister had a plan where she could call me for free five days out of the year, otherwise we just wrote letters to each other. To top it off, I had just had my second daughter a few months before. They had not even seen her. I was longing for my family. These were our "slim pickings" days. My husband cut firewood for a living and was out of work each year when the weather got too bad. We had an old pickup truck we were trying to sell. When it sold, we finally had a little extra money. My husband said we could drive down to Florida and see my family! Now a Florida vacation sounds quite extravagant. But this one wasn't. Really, it was all of my husband's worst nightmares rolled into one! My mom had bought three really awful houses, sight unseen, when she moved to Florida. She and my sister were living in the worst one, while she rented the other two out. It was a two-story garage turned into a one-bedroom apartment on each level. My mom and my and my five-year-old and three-year-old little sisters lived downstairs. My sister, brother-in-law, and her two little ones lived upstairs. There was no central heat or air-conditioning, and the place was so totally roach infested that my sister told me her family had to eat with their plates in their laps to keep the roaches out of their food!

Now one thing my husband really has a hard time with is undisciplined kids. He likes orderly rules, followed out in an orderly manner. Without getting into too much detail, let's just say it was total chaos. I imagine it was always crazy being that cramped, but adding four more people made it over the top wild. Another thing my husband really hates is being hot and cramped when he sleeps. While I was having a wonderful time seeing my family during the day, I was terrified of sleeping there at night. We each had some sort of a makeshift mattress on the floor. The first night, I felt a cockroach run across my face. I was afraid to sleep on my mattress, so I slept on top of my husband. Or I tried to sleep.

Besides of all that, someone had taken a knife and cut all my mom's window screens. She couldn't even open her windows! (She was afraid of those lizard things they have down there.) My husband graciously lived through my vacation and spent a day repairing all of my mom's screens.

After we got back home, I wracked my brain trying to come up with something I could do, to "one up" all that he had just done for me. I couldn't come up with anything! At first, I panicked realizing there was no way I could outdo what Walter had done for me. Then a new thought hit me. Walter loves me, outside of my performance, he just loves me. What if I just accepted it?

I got rid of the tally in my head. That was really freeing and a big relief. I decided he must love me, because there was no way I could pay him back!

But don't we do the same thing with God? I know I do. If I miss quiet time, or have a rotten attitude about something, or look in the mirror and just don't like what I see, I struggle to believe God loves me. Do you have a performance-based mentality? Do you try to figure out if you meet up to God standards? Do you feel more confident with God after a "good" day? I will be honest if I can actually get my whole house clean all at once, I feel good about myself, and more confident with God. Kind of crazy huh? Let's look at what Jesus did. Well first of all, He planned on redeeming us before He even created us. Next, He worked out a way to make it possible. Then He literally gave up everything for us. He totally committed and covenanted Himself to us in the face of rejection, hatred, and abuse. He held nothing back. There is nothing we could ever do to deserve what Jesus did. There is no way we could pay Him back. Maybe we ought to just let go and believe He loves us, passionately, completely without our ability to change or even totally reciprocate. Let's just relax and receive His love. Let's let Him change us. Let's believe that He started the work in us, and He will finish it. Let's quit trying to get Him to love us, and realize He already does!

Chapter 11

Jesus The Second Adam

The Bible calls Jesus the Second Adam. Adam was the progenitor of the human race. He contained the seed of every human that would ever live. When Adam died spiritually the entire human race inherited this curse of death.

Jesus was the progenitor of the born-again race. This *last Adam* (Jesus) carried the seed of every born-again person within Himself. Our faith-man was there inside of Him, in the form of the Word. We were in Him when He was judged for sin, died, and rose again. We were in Him when He was raised from the dead and set at the right hand of the Father. Jesus is the fountainhead and carrier of a whole new race of beings. Paul E Billheimer touches on this, in his excellent book *Destined for the Throne*.

"In the mind of God every believer shares complete identity with Christ from the cross to the throne. According to the Word, we are crucified with Him, buried with Him, raised with Him, exalted with Him, and enthroned with Him. How is this understandable? Consider the following: The total cumulative sin of the world could not be laid upon Him independent of the sinner himself. There is no such thing as abstract sin, sin apart from the sinner. Not only was the sinner's sin laid upon Him, but the person of the sinner as well."[34]

The Principle of Seed in Our Redemption

---

[34] Paul E. Billheimer, *Destined for the Throne*, (Minneapolis, Minnesota, Bethany House Publishers,1975) p.88

Although Billheimer doesn't explain how the person of the sinner is laid upon Jesus, I believe it is through the principle of the seed. Let's think back a minute to what we learned in Chapter 3, about how Levi paid tithes to Melchizedek many years before he was born. How did he do this? The principle of the seed.

Hebrews 7:9-10 *"And so to speak, through Abraham even Levi, who received tithes, paid tithes, for he was still in the loins of his father when Melchizedek met him."*

This strange and amazing principle helps us understand how Abraham was justified by faith. Jesus was in his loins when he believed for the supernatural birth of Isaac. So, Abraham believed for the supernatural birth of not only Isaac but of Jesus also. Also, Jesus was in the loins of Isaac when Abraham was about to sacrifice him on Mount Moriah, knowing that when he (Abraham) killed Isaac, God would have to raise him from the dead. Therefore, Abraham believed for not only Isaac's resurrection from the dead, but Jesus' also!

This principle also explains why every human being was born with a sin nature. We were all present in Adam (in his loins) when he disobeyed God and died spiritually and eventually physically. Adam not only brought about his own separation from God, but every human being that would ever be born. We were in him when he did this.

This same seed principle explains our redemption, and why we must be born-again to be saved. Jesus carried the spiritual seed of every born-again person inside Him. Just as Levi paid tithes in Abraham's loins, our spiritual seed was in Christ when he paid the price for sin, when he was resurrected and born-again.

How Jesus Dealt with the Sin Problem

This understanding of our union with Christ sheds light on a verse that was difficult for me to understand.

John 16:7-11 *"But I tell you the truth it is to your advantage that I go away; for it I do not go away, the*

Helper will not come to you; but if I go, I will send Him to you. And He when He comes, will convict the world concerning sin, and righteousness and judgement; concerning sin, because they do not believe in Me; and concerning righteousness because I go to the Father and you no longer see Me; and concerning judgement, because the ruler of this world has been judged."

These are the things the Holy Spirit convicts **the world** of, not believers but the world. This used to confuse me: *"concerning sin because they do not believe in me".* Why would the Holy Spirit convict the world of sin, because they do not believe in Jesus? Aren't sins things like don't kill, don't steal, etc.? Why would not believing in Jesus be a sin?

Remember how Jesus said *"Either make the tree good and its fruit good, or make the tree bad and its fruit bad; for the tree is known by its fruit"* (Matthew 12:13) Jesus is not dealing with the **fruit** of sin, He is dealing with the **root** of sin. The **root of sin** is that mankind is spiritually dead. The only remedy for spiritual death is to believe in Jesus! When we believe in Jesus, we are reborn a spiritually alive being. The Holy Spirit convicts the world for not believing in Jesus, because that is the only cure for sin! When we believe in Jesus our **root** changes from a root of sin to a root of God's nature. When the root changes, the fruit changes. We are united with Him!

Faith is not of this realm! It time travels!

Abraham's faith in Christ justified Him centuries ahead of time. Our faith in Christ travels back in time. It puts us inside of Jesus. Our faith united with His living Word is the substance and assurance of our new creation and our redeemed body! When you believe in Jesus you are outside of time and space. You are inside of Him when He is crucified. You are inside of Him when He goes to hell. You are inside of Him when He is raised from the dead. You are inside of Him when He is standing before the Father and Satan is standing beside Him accusing you of your sin. You are inside of Him when the Lord answers *"The Lord rebuke you Satan is this not a firebrand plucked from the fire?"* (Meaning in Christ, the debt is fully paid. You are inside of Christ Jesus the righteous! The Son whom God begot on that day!!!!) You are inside of Him as He takes His seed to a higher creation, a new creation of sons!

But those who have not believed on Jesus are still spiritually dead. They do not have the nature of God implanted within them. They need the conviction of sin to see that they are spiritually dead. They need the conviction of righteousness because they are deaf and blind to who God is. They need the conviction of judgement because they are of this world. As such they are going to be judged with the god of this world, Satan. They can either be judged with Satan or be rescued from his domain by being in Christ.

When Adam sinned, he was separated from God. This began the process of "in dying you will surely die." Death began immediately and eventually some 900 years later, he died physically.

When Jesus was raised from the dead, life was manifested in Him, spiritual life and physical eternal life. When we accept Jesus the process is reversed, in living (being made alive to God) we will surely live (get our new resurrection bodies).

How Do We Take on Jesus' DNA, otherwise known as How to We Become Born Again?

How do we become born of Jesus' own spiritual DNA? The Bible shows us how. The parable of the sower is found in three of the four gospels. It is located in Matthew 13, Mark 4, and Luke 8.

In Matthew and Mark's account immediately preceding the parable, and in Luke's directly following the parable,

Jesus is told that His mother and brothers are trying to see Him. They were unable to reach Him because of the crowd.

"Answering them, He said, 'Who are My mother and My brothers?' Looking about at those who were sitting around Him, He said, 'Behold My mother and My brothers! For whoever does the will of God, he is My brother and sister and mother." (Mark 3:33-34)

I believe this is significant to the parable of the sower. I believe Jesus then goes on to explain how we become His family. First, the sower sows the *word of the kingdom.* The word of the kingdom is the gospel as revealed in the Bible. When we hear the gospel the seed of Jesus is available to us. It is sown on different types of ground or hearts. In several places the seed does not survive due to lack of understanding, persecution, affliction, the worries of the world or the deceitfulness of riches. Then there is the good soil which produces thirty, sixty and a hundred-fold. Thirty, sixty and hundredfold of what? Of Christ being formed in us! Remember seed produces after its own kind. Literally, it reproduces the nature of Christ in us. In the spirit we began to look like Jesus, act like Jesus, smell like Jesus.

"But the seed in the good soil, these are the ones who have heard the word in an honest and good heart, and hold it fast, and bear fruit with perseverance." Luke 8:15

*"For by these He has granted to us His precious and magnificent promises, so that by them you may become partakers of the **divine nature**, having escaped the corruption that is in the world by lust."* 2 Peter 1:4

*"And the **seed** whose **fruit is righteousness** is sown in peace by those who make peace."* James 3:18 Think about that, there is a seed that if you plant it, it will produce righteousness. Of course, we have already been talking about this. It is the gospel. It is a seed that produces Christ. It produces righteousness.

"Do not lie to one another, since you have laid aside the old self with its evil practices, and have put on the new

169

*self who is being renewed to a true knowledge according to the **image of the One who created him.**"* Colossians 3:9-10

Do you see it? The Word of God is the seed of Christ. It changes our (spiritual) makeup, our constitution. There is a genetic transformation taking place. How about this verse? "*But we all with unveiled face, beholding in a mirror the glory of the Lord, are being transformed into the same image, from glory to glory, just as from the Lord, the Spirit.* "2 Corinthians 3:18

I will be honest with you, that verse used to make no sense to me at all. And then after I got this revelation, it hit me. When you look in a mirror, what are you looking at? Your own image. You are looking at yourself, your identity. When we look in the mirror in this verse what do we see? We see Jesus! As we see Him, we are transformed into His image. As we see ourselves in His identity, we start "looking" more and more like Him.

This is Jesus description of how we become His family and take on His nature. I have heard the Parable of the Sower used to teach on many different things, and I don't think it is necessarily wrong, just slightly out of context. The purpose of the seed in our lives is to cause a rebirth of our spirit, so that we are that new creation with Christ's nature. We become the same species and likeness of Christ. Jesus is a spiritually alive human and we are too.

I Corinthians 15: 45,49-50 "*So also it is written, 'The first man, Adam, became a living soul.' the last Adam became a life-giving spirit ...Just as we have borne the image of the earthy, we will also bear the image of the heavenly. Now I say this, brethren, that flesh and blood cannot inherit the kingdom of God, nor does the perishable inherit the imperishable.*"

We bear the image of Adam in our physical body, now. But spiritually we bear the image of Jesus, and at the resurrection our physical bodies will leave that old image behind for good, and bear the image of Christ. We will have an imperishable body.

Adam a type of Christ

Of the many types and shadows of Jesus in the Old Testament, one of my favorites is Adam. Adam is a type of Christ as he is naming all the animals. He can find no help meet suitable for him. Of all the animals, there is none of the same species or kind to be his mate. He could have searched the animal kingdom for eternity, but he was on a higher level than the animals. Adam was made in the image of God. He needed a help meet of this higher creation. God causes a deep sleep (a type of death) to come on him. Out of Adam's side, God forms his bride.

This is a type of Jesus. He could not find a help meet, a bride, any of His own kind.

Psalm 53:2-3 *"God has looked down from heaven upon the sons of men, to see if there is anyone who understands, who seeks after God. Every one of them has turned aside; together they have become corrupt; there is no one who does good, not even one."* Jesus was of a higher order than mankind. There was no one like Him. God caused the deep sleep of death to fall on Jesus and out of His side as the blood and water flowed, the church was formed. Jesus our second Adam's own bride was birthed out of His suffering, out of His side.

Ron Wyatt's Discovery

There is a very interesting man, now passed away, named Ron Wyatt. You can find out about him at wyattmuseum.com or anchorstone.com. He was just a normal guy. He worked as an anesthesiologist. But on his time off, he was like a real-life Indiana Jones. He and his sons made many trips to the Holy Land and found the real sites to many Bible events. For instance, he found the Red Sea crossing site, and even found the coral covered remains of chariot wheels on the bottom of the sea! He found the real Mt. Sinai, the rock that the water flowed out of, and the altar made for the golden calf. The most amazing of all his discoveries was the Ark of the Covenant!

Through some supernatural leading, He knew where to look and got permission to do so. First, he found an early church structure, near the crucifixion site. Then he found the actual holes that the crosses were put into. Eventually he excavated and found an underground cavern with the articles from the temple.

The ark and temple treasures are believed to have been hidden from the Babylonians by the prophet Jeremiah, just before Jerusalem was attacked and the inhabitants taken into exile. Inside the cavern, Ron Wyatt found a stone box. The ark of the covenant was hidden inside! (I am telling the story quickly, but I don't want to take away from the amazing account found on the website.) The stone case was directly beneath the cross where Jesus was crucified. (Below about 20 feet of stone). And, likely during the earthquake that occurred while Jesus was on the cross, the bedrock was cracked all the way through! The lid of the stone case enclosing the ark of the covenant was also cracked.

At Jesus' crucifixion, when that Roman soldier thrust his spear into Jesus side and the blood and water poured out....it fell down through the cracked rock ...down into the secret cavern that Jeremiah found hundreds of years earlier...through the cracked stone lid. The blood of Jesus fell on the mercy seat of the Ark of the Covenant! No human hand touched the blood, and yet, in the providence of God, Jesus, the perfect sacrifice, our Passover lamb, poured out His blood on the Mercy Seat.

Our Savior, the Progenitor of the born-again race, made propitiation for our sins and birthed His bride from a wound in His side, as He was in the deep sleep of death. The second Adam birthed us. And we are a new species.

"Therefore, if anyone is in Christ, he is a new creature, the old things passed away, behold new things have come." 2 Corinthians 5:17

There is a passage of scripture in Hebrews chapter two quoted from Psalms chapter eight.

"What is Man, that you remember Him? Or the son of man that You are concerned about Him? You have made Him for a little while lower than the angels; You have crowned him with glory and honor, and have appointed him over the works of Your hands; You have put all things in subjection under his feet."

In Hebrews, the author then goes on to talk about Jesus and how this refers to Him. My question always was: is this verse just talking about Jesus or mankind in general? I couldn't figure it out. But then I realized, it is both Jesus and mankind in Christ. What Jesus accomplished as man, He accomplished for us. It is Jesus as man, coming and being lower than the angels with us, then while carrying us inside of Him, as His seed, crowned with glory and honor, and appointed over the work of His hands. Mankind is raised to a new level. In Christ we are a higher creation.

My Jesus Suit

About eight years ago, I was praying. As I sat there for just a brief moment, I had a picture of myself inside of Jesus. Like I was encased in Him.

My kids had gone to summer camp several years before. While at camp they played this silly game. The camp had two giant, blow-up, sumo wrestler suits. The kids would put them on and run into each other and bounce off of each other. It was just goofy, but my mini-vision reminded me of that, so I called it my 'Jesus suit revelation'. I thought I had better research and find out if my 'Jesus suit' was in the Bible.

"For all of you who were baptized into Christ have clothed yourselves with Christ." Galatian 3:27

"But put on (as a garment) *the Lord Jesus Christ, and make no provision for the flesh in regard to its lusts."* Romans 13:14

Both of these verses talk about putting Jesus on as a covering or clothing. Roland Buck talks about the atonement in the book *Angels on Assignment,* (the atonement might be another term for "the Jesus suit").

"God cannot tolerate sin because of His very nature. From His viewpoint there must be total perfection before He can accept us. From our earthly viewpoint, we look for a way to make ourselves free from sin by pulling ourselves up by our own boot straps, but God explained holiness to me in an entirely new light.

Holiness is very similar to the glory of God. It is the outraying of His personality and His presence. Absence of sin is the *result* of *holiness,* not holiness itself. Holiness is literally the character and nature of God.

GOD IS HOLY!

God speaks of the highway of holiness which reaches right down to earth. Through grace, God's unmerited favor, man approaches God on that highway. Jesus was and is the holiness of God extended to us, and He provides the way because He IS the way! We are accepted by God because Jesus was holy, and then we are covered with righteousness so that GOD SEES US EXACTLY LIKE HE SEES JESUS! "[35]

---

[35] Charles and Frances Hunter, *Angels on Assignment*, (Houston, TX. Hunter Books, 1979) p.112

Old Testament Types of Our Jesus Suit
The Red Sea

As you know I love the Old Testament pictures of these truths. When I think of "the Jesus suit" two Old Testament types come to mind. The first is the Pillar of Cloud and Fire that followed the children of Israel as they left Egypt heading for the Promised Land.

1 Corinthians 10:1-2 says *"For I do not want you to be unaware, brethren that our fathers were all under the cloud and all passed through the sea; and all were baptized into Moses in the cloud and in the sea;"*

Also keeping in mind, *"For all of you who were baptized into Christ have clothed yourselves with Christ."* Galatians 3:26.

We see the Israelites Red Sea crossing is a type of our baptism and being clothed with Christ. Baptism is a type of death and a rite of passage from an old identity into a new identity.

Roman 6:3-4 explains the significance of baptism. *"Or do you not know that all of us who have been baptized into Christ Jesus have been baptized into His death? Therefore, we have been buried with Him through baptism into death, so that as Christ was raised from the dead through the glory of the Father, so we too might walk in newness of life,"*

The children of Israel were a clan of slaves. They were victims. They were the lowest of Egyptians. When they passed through the sea, this was the point of no turning back to Egypt. This was their death to the old life. They were no longer even on the continent of Egypt; they were no longer Egyptian slaves! They were reborn as a nation, God's nation! They were covered by the cloud and the fire, a type of the atonement or the "Jesus suit". God overshadowed them. His identity covered them. Just think, their bondage, the Pharaoh's army, also was baptized into the Red Sea! So, we see the baptism is not just a "type" of death, it is a type of judgement **and** death. Their bondage perished in the sea, while they were covered by the cloud and came out on the other side free and victorious over their bondage!

When we are baptized into Christ's death, we are **in** Christ. The judgement of hell fell on our covering. The sin was judged. We came out of the waters of baptism just as Jesus came out of the fiery baptism of judgement. The judgement fell on Jesus, who became our sin. We came out free from our bondage to sin and guilt. We have a new identity and a new homeland. A new King and a new God! We are clothed with the "cloud" who is Jesus and bear His identity.

Noah's Ark

The second Old Testament event that represents the "Jesus suit" was Noah's ark. This *type* is also associated with baptism. And remember those of us who are baptized into Christ are clothed with Christ.

"*...who once were disobedient when the patience of God kept waiting in the days of Noah, during the construction of the ark, in which a few, that is eight persons, were brought through the water. Corresponding to that, baptism now saves you-not the removal of dirt from the flesh, but an appeal to God for a good conscience-through the resurrection of Jesus Christ.*" 1 Peter 3:20-21.

There are some really exciting types in this story. First of all, the word for pitch is actually the word for atone.

"*...and shall cover it inside and out with pitch*" Genesis 6:14.

In Hebrew this literally says "*you shall atone, make propitiation of it, inside and outside with the ransom, the price of a life*"

The ark is a type of Christ and a type of the atonement or "Jesus suit"! It was covered with the ransom of a life. The waters of judgement beat upon Christ, while we were

176

safe inside. He carried us out of judgement. There were eight people in the ark. Eight is the number of new beginnings and also the number associated with Jesus. The ark came to rest on Mount Ararat on the same day of the year, Nissan seventeen, that Jesus was raised from the dead! So, you can see this represents the judgement of sin and the resurrection of the dead. The name Ararat means: the curse reversed! Isn't that what Jesus accomplished for us? He reversed the curse of death brought on by Adam. He carried us inside of Him to a new beginning, to a place of fellowship with God. Noah and his family passed through the judgement waters of the flood. Then they had a new beginning. A new beginning for mankind built from their family. Noah and his family were "in Christ" and safe from judgement.

A Progressive Revelation of the "Jesus suit"

My "Jesus suit" revelation was a progressive revelation. At first it meant freedom from the bondage of my own negative self-identity. A big one for me is being embarrassed. This ties in with pride. When I was younger, embarrassment was so much a part of my life, that the first time I heard it was possible **not** to be embarrassed, I was shocked. It was such a new idea to me. As a matter of fact, the possibility hadn't even occurred to me before.

It happened when my husband was still my fiancé. He was attending Rhema Bible Training Center. I was across the country at a school in North Carolina. Walter called me and told me of an incident that happened in his class at Rhema. The classroom was quite large. When Brother Hagin taught, it would be the whole group of either first- or second-year students. As Walter was listening to Brother Hagin teach, he noticed that he had a lady's hair clip in his hair. As time went on, more and more students noticed and started giggling and whispering to one another. Brother Hagin noticed and put his hand on his head and felt the clip. He took it off and explained to the class that his hair was sticking up funny that morning. His wife had wetted his hair and put one of her clips in it to hold it down while it dried. He had forgotten all about it until the class started laughing.

Then Brother Hagin said, "I suppose you all think I am embarrassed. I'm not. I don't get embarrassed."

When Walter related the story to me, I was pretty awestruck. It was the first time I realized it was a possibility to live free from embarrassment.

To be honest, at first my "Jesus suit" was an escape from *my* negative self-image to *Jesus'* image. I could look in the mirror either literally or in my imagination and picture Jesus. But as time went on, I realized it was so much deeper than that. Our identity in Christ is much the same as Jesus' identity was the Father, when He walked the earth!

At the end of His life Jesus had this conversation with His disciples.

"Jesus said to him, 'I am the way, and the truth and the life; no one comes to the Father but through Me. If you had known Me, you would have known My Father also, from now on you know Him, and have seen Him.'

Philip said to Him, 'Lord, show us the Father, and it is enough for us."

Jesus said to him, 'Have I been so long with you, and yet you have not come to know Me, Philip? He who has seen Me has seen the Father, how can you say;" Show us the Father?" Do you not believe that I am in the Father, and the Father is in Me? The words that I say to you, I do not speak on My own initiative, but the Father abiding in Me does His works…"

Jesus was shocked that they still didn't understand Him. He had been showing them the Father the whole time. He had completely laid aside His own will and identity. Everything He had done was according to the Father's plan. It was done in obedience to the Father. He had totally aligned Himself in will, purpose, and expression to the Father. You could say Jesus had the Father's nature and obeyed His will. Everything Jesus did was an expression of the Father!

How could Philip say "Show us the Father," when that is what He had been doing the whole time?

Hebrews 1:3 says Jesus is the **exact** representation of His nature. That is what we are to be: an exact representation of Jesus' nature. We are to lay aside our agenda. We are to lay aside selfish promotion, which is pretty much our identity. That is what baptism is! We die to the selfish use of our own mind, will and emotions (soul) and our bodies. They are now submitted to Jesus to be a representation of His will.

In Matthew 16:24-25 Jesus says "*Then Jesus said to His disciples, 'If anyone wishes to come after Me, he must deny himself, and take up his cross and follow Me, For whoever wishes to save his life will lose it, but whoever loses his life for My sake will find it.'*"

What is Jesus saying here? What does it mean to take up your cross? The cross was the ultimate act of the laying down of Jesus' will. We have to lay aside our own will to take up His. Do you know the context of this verse? Jesus was telling the disciples that He was going to die. Peter took Jesus aside and said "*God forbid, Lord! This shall never happen to you.*" Although Peter was trying to be compassionate, he was wrong. The easy way wasn't the best way.

Jesus rebuked him. He said "*Get behind Me, Satan!*" Jesus could not afford to entertain even the notion of His own self-preservation.

When I think of this topic, I think of a verse that I have heard quoted hundreds of times, and yet very rarely, maybe once or twice, have I ever heard the whole verse quoted!

It is Revelation 12:11 "*And they overcame him* (Satan), *by the blood of the Lamb, and by the word of their testimony, and **they loved not their lives unto the death**.*" (KJV) Listen next time you hear that verse, you will be surprised that no one finishes it! Yes, we overcome by the blood and the word of our testimony, but there is a third important component here. We cannot love our life! We have to lay it down!

James 4:7 reinforces this: "**Submit** *therefore to God, Resist the devil and he will flee from you.*" The Greek word for submit there is *hupotasso*. It means to place rank under, be subjected to, obey. How many times have we heard, "Resist the devil and he will flee from you?" That is not what it says. First, we must submit to God! We need to place ourselves in obedience to Him, then we resist the devil and he will flee.

How to Die

I remember a time quite a few years ago, I got in an argument with my adult daughter. I got so angry with her I lashed out and yelled some awful things at her. Afterward I went for a jog around our local park. As I was jogging, I was asking God how not to be angry. I thought I should apologize, but I was so angry that I was just churning inside. "How do I not be angry?" I asked God.

I felt Him answer pretty clearly "You die."

The really sad thing is that I didn't know how to die. I had been a Christian many years. I really felt like the Lord had answered me, but I didn't know how to die. Looking back, I can see the problem now. I focused on the issue at hand. I tried not to feel my feelings, but I was just as angry every time I thought about it. I was trying to lay my life down for my daughter in the situation. I was thinking about what was fair. Now these many years later, I can see my error. We lay our life down for Jesus. We lay what is fair down for Jesus. We focus on Him. We say something like: "*Jesus, I lay down my right to what is fair for You. You didn't have things fair. You went to hell for me. That wasn't fair. You had to lay aside everything for me. That wasn't fair. I submit to You. I love you. I lay aside my natural reactions so that Your nature can flow through me*". I am being really specific, because that is what I needed: really specific directions on how to die.

Did you know there is a portion of scripture that talks about this? There is! I had never noticed it before, which is awful because it is a part of a scripture I had memorized and quoted many times. I had never read the context! Well, I read it. I just never **perceived** it. The text I am talking about is 1 Peter chapter two. I would really recommend reading the whole book through and follow the topic. It is about learning to love when it isn't fair! I don't want to write the whole chapter. I will pick out some key verses to follow the flow of thought.

"Since you have in obedience to the truth purified your souls for a sincere love of the brethren, fervently love one another from the heart, for you have been born again not of seed which is perishable, but imperishable, that is through the living and enduring word of God" 1 Peter 1:22-23 (There is our seed theme again!)

"Beloved, I urge you as aliens and strangers to abstain from fleshly lusts which wage war against the soul. Keep your behavior excellent among the Gentiles, so that in the thing in which they slander you as evildoers, they may because of your good deeds, as they observe them, glorify God in the day of visitation." 1 Peter 2:11-12

*"For this finds favor, if for the **sake of conscience toward God** a person bears up under sorrows when **suffering unjustly**. For what credit is there if, when you sin and are harshly treated, you endure it with patience? But if when **you do what is right** and **suffer** for it you patiently endure it; this finds favor with God. **For you have been called for this purpose**,* (we have been called for the purpose of laying down our lives and suffering unjustly!) *since Christ also suffered for you, leaving you an example for you to follow in His steps, who committed no sin, nor was any deceit found in His mouth; and while being reviled, He did not revile in return; while suffering, He uttered no threats, **but kept entrusting Himself to Him** who judges righteously; and He himself*

181

bore our sins in His body on the cross, so that we might die to sin and live to righteousness; for by His wounds you were healed. "1 Peter 2:19-25

This well-known healing verse is saying, when Jesus unjustly bore our sins and wounds, He brought us healing. His unjust treatment brought us healing. When we bear things unjustly, we will minister Jesus to others! It even says **this is the purpose** we were called to! We are to follow Jesus example. I love the part that says, "*But kept entrusting Himself to Him.*" That's important, God is the focus here, not the injustice. We do it for Him. We lay down our lives for Him. The next chapter starts with ..." *In the same way.* What way? Bearing things unjustly,." *you wives be submissive to your own husbands.*" Then farther down in verse seven, "*You husbands **in the same way, live** with your wives in an understanding way…*" Are you seeing what I see? God is telling us things aren't going to be fair, they are going to be **un**fair, but love anyway! Lay down your life for others just like Jesus did for you. When He did it you were healed, follow His example and show Jesus to others.

When I was studying this, I felt like I was starting to get this, but still wasn't seeing things as clearly as I wanted to. Then my sister just happened to give me a book by Nancy Missler that really helped me to understand these concepts. Actually, there are two books by Nancy Missler that really helped me. *Why Should I be the First to Change* tells Nancy's personal story, and *The Way of Agape* is an in-depth Bible study on learning how to die to our own self and let God's love flow out to others. I highly recommend both books. In *Why Should I be the First to Change,* Nancy tells the story of her marriage to Chuck Missler, at first a successful businessman and then a well-known Bible teacher. Although they were both Christians and even Bible teachers, their marriage had come to a breaking point. Nancy was going to leave in two days' time. In one final conversation or argument with Chuck, Nancy realized she had spent years trying to change her husband, but never considered changing herself! It was then God gave her a revelation of how selfish she was, too. Her sinful attitudes were mostly a reaction to what seemed to be rejection by her husband, but they blocked God's nature from being able to come forth in her life. Nancy had a revelation of how to die to herself, even sacrificially, and let God's divine nature come through. Because she writes with such transparency and clarity, my questions were answered. I finally could see how to die, and how to live! Her life, although much more dramatic than my own, was my story too! I have spent so many years waiting for my circumstances, family members, husband, church etc. etc. to get in line so that I could feel okay, have some peace, feel loved and accepted. I, like Nancy, was full of repressed anger, fear and selfishness! Mostly because I didn't know what to do with my feelings. I knew they were wrong; I just didn't know how to get rid of them.

Nancy says, **"So what I needed to learn at that time was how to recognize the things in my life that blocked and sealed off God's love in my heart and how to give those things over to Him, moment by moment …I didn't simply bury my real feelings like I used to, or pretend they weren't there. I just kept recognizing them as they came up and verbally handing them over to God, thus allowing God's love (which was already in my heart) to continue to come forth."**[36] I know on paper the difference between burying feelings and handing them over to God sounds minor, but in reality, it is HUGE! It is the difference between bondage and freedom. We do NOT have to be in bondage to our emotions and feelings, even ones that seem justified! We surrender them in obedience to Jesus, just as He surrendered to the Father!

---

[36] Nancy Missler, Why Should I be the First to Change (Coeur d' Alene, ID, King's High way Ministries, Inc.,) p.94,96

I have an example that seems a little different, but it is actually the same thing! A few years back my twin sister was diagnosed with cancer of her uterus. The doctor was going to give her a hysterectomy and then determine if anything else needed to be done. I decided I was going to pray and get ahold of God in faith. I got alone in my room and tried to pray. Instead, all I could do is think about what my life would be like without my sister. Before long, I was sobbing and my heart felt like it was breaking in two! The woman of faith somehow turned into a pitiful, filled with self-pity, useless heap! My son heard me and came into my room. "Please get Dad!" I managed to say between sobs. I thought my husband would come and comfort me.

He came into the room. Once he found out why I was crying, he said without even a hint of pity, "Well, tell your emotions to get in line with the Word of God!"

I was kind of shocked at my husband's callous attitude, but I said out loud "Emotions, get in line with the Word of God." I was surprised. The grief and pain immediately left! I was able to pray. My sister was fine. She had the hysterectomy, but nothing else was needed. The doctor was worried about the surgery, because of some previous surgeries she had, had, but everything went well. I learned an important lesson, even self-pity, fear, and worry, fall into the category of sinful attitudes! We can be free from them. We can submit them to God. I don't know that if I would have continued to wallow in my self-pity, if it would have affected my sister's healing or not. But I know for sure that until I dealt with it, my prayers would have done no good!

The paradox of the Christian life is: we are living in two realms. As a born-again creation, born of the seed of the second Adam, Jesus Christ, our loyalties are not to this physical realm. We have this physical body that is contrary to the reality of who we really are. We are still carrying around the carcass we inherited from the first Adam. We live by faith and the nature of the second

Adam is who we truly are. That nature of Jesus, the Divine nature is born of faith, lived by faith, and comes to maturity by faith. The substance of the new man is the Word of God coming into contact with the faith of our hearts. As long as we hold on to that Word in faith, something is growing and increasing inside of us, in the spirit realm. That something is Christ! This life is never going to be about me, my identity, who I am. It is always going to be "Christ in me the hope of glory."

Chapter 12

Who Am I?

What are the implications of Christ Jesus the Man? How does His humanity change us and our identity?

This is momentous! Who Christ is defines who we **are**! Just as much as the fall of Adam defined who we **were**. We are now recreated to be of the race of Christ, sons of the Living God! *"For you are all sons of God through faith in Christ Jesus"* Galatians 3:26

Let's remember that we are a three part being. We are predominantly a spiritual creature who possesses a soul and lives in a body. Our spirit is the essence of who we are. Our soul is the expression and connection between the spirit and the body. It can be influenced by either or even predominate over both.

It is the spiritual part of man that has been born-again. In that realm where faith creates reality, where the essence and the material are not separate. (Remember we talked about this. In the spirit realm we can see and smell things like thankfulness or worship or even the stench of envy or gossip.) This is where the new birth takes place. This is where we literally become a new species. We are born of the Word of God by faith. This is the spiritual DNA, seed, or the nature of Christ implanted within us. This is more than an attitude change or a paradigm change. This is a species change! This is why a criminal can become a minister, or a shy, timid, person a bold preacher.

This reminds me of a true story I heard many years ago on the radio program *Focus on The Family*. A Christian woman was abducted by a murderer. He got into her car and held her at gunpoint. The woman felt moved to pray for this man. She found out later he had killed a woman earlier that day and would have most likely killed her. But she told him how God loved him. The man couldn't even relate to what love was. She asked him, "Is there anything at all you care about?" He said he did have a son. She shared how God felt for him, like he did for his son. She led him to the Lord, gave him her Bible and dropped him off at bus station. She informed the police about it. They were ready to arrest him, when the bus got to its destination. When the police found him, he was studying the Bible! He surrendered peacefully, and the only thing he asked for was to talk to the lady who told him about Jesus! This is the miracle of the new birth!

The Nature of Seed in the Universe

When Adam sinned, the human race was no longer capable of intimacy with God. The entire race was lowered in every way. We became sickly, mortal, vain, foolish, selfish, etc... We had the nature of PRIDE. We were of our father Adam and his god, Satan who is the author of pride, rebellion, and lies. If you think back to the first few chapters of this book, we learned that God made us in the sixth day of creation. Creation requires the genetic information of God's will for each individual creation. That information is stored in the DNA or seed. The parent seed carried all the information for every tree, plant, animal and person. If you can go back to thinking in the quantum realm, as we did in chapter one, this whole material realm that we know of as reality is just a vast sea of vibration and energy. It is held together in brilliant design. Reality, as we know it, is energy held together by what we know to be the thoughts and faith of God. So, the center point of reality is information. Specifically, it is information from the mind of God the Father programed into creation. It is God's design. It is written in every cell of your body. It is DNA. God in His incredibly beautiful mind imagined every detail of the time-space continuum. He placed the information into creation. That is how you were created six thousand years ago. Adam carried your information, your blueprint.

The physicist, astronomer and mathematician James Jeans is quoted, **"I incline to the idealistic theory that consciousness is fundamental, and that the material universe is derivative from consciousness, not consciousness from the material universe... In general, the universe seems to me to be nearer to a great thought than to a great machine. It may well be, it seems to me, that each individual consciousness ought to be compared to a brain-cell in a universal mind."[37]**

Indeed, I think scripture confirms the universe **is** a great thought, from our Creator's great mind. He has programmed the information for His thought into the seed. As we have learned through this book, history could be called the Battle of the Seed. The seed is God's plan. It was corrupted at the very beginning of man's history. We inherited that corrupted seed.

Mankind was hopelessly lost and doomed to damnation (eternal separation from God). God devised a plan in which He could be just, and yet still redeem this seed corrupted race. He made a way for us to be born of seed that cannot be corrupted! We were born of His own seed.

*"Since you have in obedience to the truth purified your souls for a sincere love of the brethren, fervently love one another from the heart, **for you have been born again not of seed which is perishable but imperishable, that is, through the living and enduring word of God**."* (1 Peter 1:23)

I heard someone say once that in heaven you are not separate from your words. They are a part of you. Jesus was TRUTH. He spoke TRUTH. He lived and acted TRUTH. Jesus said *"It is the Spirit who gives life, the*

---

[37] James Jeans, *Physics and Philosophy*, (Courier Corporation, 1981) p.216 (cited from Wikipedia, James Jeans)

flesh profits nothing; the **words** *that I have spoken to you are spirit and are life."* John 6:63

Jesus is the Word of God. Jesus spoke the Word of God. Jesus acted out the Word of God. When we receive that Word by faith, we are receiving Jesus, Himself and His nature.

God didn't fix the old seed. He gave us a new seed. That is why we can't fix our old nature; we just have to die to it. Then we learn to live out of the new nature that is in our spirit.

"For those whom He foreknew, He also predestined to become conformed to the image of His Son, so that He would be the firstborn among many brethren;" Romans 8:29

The Seed of Abraham

Let's think back to the Seed of Abraham. How was Isaac born? He was born when Abraham believed God's promise. God's word, mixed with Abraham's faith, produced a child. Isaac is both a type of Christ and a carrier of the seed of Messiah. Christ in Abraham and Isaac was their hope of glory. Next how was Jesus born? The Word was spoken to Mary. It was combined with her faith when she responded *"May it be done to me according to your word."* Then she conceived that miracle child, by the Word of God's promise. Christ in her was her (and all mankind's) hope of glory. How are you born again? The Word, the promise, the gospel is combined with faith in your heart. Christ's nature is birthed in your spirit. Christ in you becomes your hope of glory! In a sense that miracle birth is recreated in the spirit of every born-again Believer!

Not only is Christ in us, but we are in Him. Jesus the Man carried that new race inside of Him. He carried you inside of Him. You were present in Christ when He was judged! You were in Him when he carried the penalty for sin. When His blood became the perfect redemption, you were inside Him. When He overcame death, when He rose victorious....

We were inside of Him when the Father said to Him, *"Thou art my Son, today I have begotten Thee."* This makes us a race of sons!!!! Those words were spoken to The Man and the race He carried!

We were in Christ when the Father said, *"Sit at My right hand until I make your enemies a footstool beneath your feet."* This is our place!

We were in Christ when the Father said to Him, *"Ask of Me and I will give the nations for your inheritance."* We should be asking!

We were in Christ when the Father said *"You are a priest forever according to the order of Melchizedek."* This makes us a race of priests!

It was of Christ and the race He carried that scripture says, *"What is man, that You remember him? Or the son of man, that You are concerned about him? You have made him for a little while lower than the angels; You have crowned him with glory and honor, and have appointed him over the works of Your hands; You have put all things in subjection under his feet."* Hebrews 2:6-8

Jesus lowered Himself so that we could be elevated! He is our identity. We are no longer sons of pride and rebellion. We are sons of Christ...of submission and humility. This is the new man in the spirit realm. This treasure is in a jar of clay, in an Adam suit. We are living in the old death body, but that is NOT who we are. We have died to Adam's nature and have taken on the nature of Christ.

Do you see it? Mankind is below the angels. He is inferior to them. But in Christ we are raised to a higher level of creation. Your standing is Christ's standing. He has raised you to a higher level. Satan's deception leads to damnation, but **Christ in you is the hope of glory**!

The New Covenant

In an earlier chapter we talked about Abraham's covenant with God. This was the Old Covenant. It was carried on by Isaac and Jacob and then through Moses the entire nation of Israel. It was based on God's infallible promises. He promised to make Abraham a great nation. He promised him the land of Israel. He promised to bless Abraham's descendants, and He promised a Seed in whom all the nations of the earth would be blessed. That Old Covenant was between Abraham and God. The God side of the covenant was ironclad. Israel's side however was a problem. Their history is riddled with failure. So much so, that instead of a blessing they fell under a curse.

Hebrews 8:6 tells about the new covenant. "*But now He (Jesus) has obtained a more excellent ministry, by as much as He is also the mediator of a better covenant, which has been enacted on better promises*"

The Old Covenant was between God and Abraham and then the entire nation of Israel under the Levitical priesthood. The New Covenant is between the Father and The Man, Jesus Christ. It is an infallible covenant, based on two infallible partners!

Just yesterday, as I was contemplating this subject, I just happened to listen to Neville Johnson's Word for the Week, while washing my dishes. He taught on praying in tongues and its importance. He also shared something I had never heard before. The correlation of circumcision and praying in tongues. It was a missing piece to my puzzle! Circumcision was the sign of the Old Covenant, whereas speaking in tongues is the sign and seal of the New Covenant.

Abraham came out of the Babylonian system. The pagan Babylonian religion is the foundation of all pagan false religions. This foul belief system worshipped sex and phallic symbols and sacrificed their children to false gods. Immorality was part of the worship. Abraham was set apart for God. He and his seed were to be holy. An important part of Abraham's covenant was protecting his seed. They were not to intermarry with the people that inhabited the land. Ezra 9:2 says *"Indeed, the Israelites have taken some of their daughters as wives for themselves and their sons, so that the **holy seed has been mixed** with the people of the land. And the leaders and officials have taken the lead in this unfaithfulness!"* (Berean Study Bible)

Their mandate was to keep pure and to keep their physical offspring pure. For they were pregnant, so to speak, with the Messiah. The sign of this covenant was circumcision. This was marking the very place where the seed issues forth as separate to God.

The New Covenant is a spiritual covenant. The spiritual seed is marked in the New Covenant. The sower sows **the word.** In the New Covenant the words we speak are the spiritual seed. God has set our mouth and communication apart for Himself. James 3:2 says *"For we all stumble in many ways. If anyone does not stumble in what he says, he is a perfect man, able to bridle the whole body as well."* The seal or sign of our redemption is the Holy Spirit, and He has marked our mouth, where the seed issues forth! What we speak is so important. It is so important God gave us a hotline to the Holy Spirit, to be able to speak forth His will and words without interference from our minds. Just as the Old Covenant marked as Holy the "seed" of the nation of Israel. The New Covenant marks the spiritual seed that we issue forth: our words. We are sowers of the Word.

Evidence of the New Creation

So, we can see that we are now a new creation. We are spirit beings that are alive to God. We are growing and developing the nature of Christ in our spirit man. This whole realm is invisible to the physical eye. It is a life of faith. It is learning to be dependent on God. Jesus showed us what our life is supposed to look like. It is a life lived in total submission and total faith in God. He also gave us a paternity test to be able to discern who is born of God and who is not.

"By this all men will know that you are My disciples, if you have love for one another" John 13:35

*"Beloved let us love one another, for love is from God, and everyone who loves is **born** of God and knows God. The one who does not love does not know God for God is love."* 1John 4:7-8

If we are born again and have the nature of God, it is going to show up. What is it going to look like? It is going to look like love. If there is no evidence of love in our lives, we had better examine what is going on and make some adjustments.

I live in a tourist town. We have a huge Cherry Festival every year. I usually avoid the traffic and don't go, but the years I have gone, I have been troubled by a group of Christians that come. They hold up signs about judgement and try to engage people in what they consider evangelism. The thing that immediately jumped out at me (and other Christians that have seen them) is their shocking lack of love! Their demeanor is one of judgement. I had a friend who kindly tried to share with them, that if they would show some love for people, that people would be more likely to respond to the gospel. This group got so angry and nasty to my friend, he had to find a policeman! Jesus warned us about this. He said *"Beware of the false prophets, who come to you in sheep's clothing, but inwardly are ravenous wolves. You will know them by their fruits. Grapes are not gathered from thorn bushes, nor figs from thistles, are they?"* (Matthew 7:15-16) I have learned this lesson from some bad experiences. If you think you are going to the "happening" meetings, lots of supernatural stuff going on, but there is no love or compassion for people, only a stroking of the leader's ego, **run,** don't walk for the door! You do not want to be there. It was the same with this group. They seemed like they wanted to get people saved, but they had no compassion for them! The seed of God produces after its own kind. A love seed produces the fruit of love.

We are in Christ

I like to look at patterns in the Bible. For approximately 2000 years starting with Abraham, the nation of Israel "carried" the physical seed of Messiah. They were in a sense "pregnant" with Him. Now in this church age. Messiah is carrying our spiritual seed. The seed for our redeemed body. He is pregnant with us, in the same sense that Israel was pregnant with Him.

I heard a minister say that we are in two places at the same time! We are here on this earth and we are "*seated with Christ in heavenly places*".   The Bible also says our citizenship is in heaven. It doesn't say it is going to be in heaven. It says it **is** in heaven right now! A citizen is entitled to the rights, privileges and protection of his home country. Most of all the citizen has a right to be **in** his home country. Colossians 3:1 says something strange. "*Therefore, **if you have been raised up with Christ**, keep seeking the things above, where Christ is, seated at the right hand of God.*"   Are we already raised up with Christ? How can that be? Aren't we living on this earth? How is it that we are already citizens of heaven?

Colossians 3:3-4 goes on to say "*For you have died and your life is hidden **with** Christ in God. When Christ, who is our life, is revealed, then you also will be revealed **with** Him in glory.*"

The word '*with*" in both of those verses is defined **"syn (a primitive preposition, having no known etymology) properly, identified *with*, joined close *together* in**

tight identification, with (=closely identified together)"[38]

So, this verse says *"For you have died and your life is hidden, joined in identity with Christ in God. When Christ, who is our life is revealed, then you also will be revealed, joined in identity with Him in glory."*

If we want to know our identity, we do not need to look at our past; it is dead. We don't have to look at our genetics; we died to them. We don't have to look at ourselves. We look at Jesus. He has covered us. He is our identity. We are who He is. We have His authority. We have His righteousness. We are being changed by the Holy Spirit and the Word of God into His image. We are everything that Jesus is!

Am I saying that we are God?

Absolutely NOT! We are not capable of even existing or holding the substance of our being together without God. God is. That is the foundation of our existence. *"Apart from Him we can do nothing"*! **In Him**, we become everything that He is. He covers us with His identity, His nature, His accomplishment. He as a man, did what we could never do: He fulfilled the law. He obeyed God completely. He submitted His will and trusted God with total faith.

The Story of Ruth

The other day my husband and I had a whole conversation without ever actually saying the words. It was not an important conversation. It was a teasing one He looked at me and I knew what he was going to say. We both knew what I would respond, so we both laughed. I said "It is funny how we just had a conversation without saying a word." He agreed. We

---

[38] Helps Word-studies, 1987,2011, Helps Ministries Inc., https://biblehub.com/greek/4862.htm

have thirty-eight years of shared thoughts and experiences together and many similar conversations.

I have other people that no matter how hard I try to communicate, I know they have no clue what I am saying. To be honest, I usually try to avoid talking to those people because it seems fruitless and frustrating.

Usually the people we can connect with have similar backgrounds and experiences, so it is like you're speaking the same language from the same alphabet, like my husband and I. Another example from my life, I was a homeschool mom with four kids. If I got around another homeschool mom with multiple kids, we had plenty to talk about. We didn't have to work for conversation. Our similar experiences made communication easy.

God is like that too. The more you know of His Word, the easier it is to communicate with Him. The more shared thoughts, the deeper the communication. This is why I feel it is important to read the whole Bible, not just the New Testament. All those Old Testament stories, besides being interesting and easy to read, are experiences you are sharing with God. The more you know them, the more you begin to develop a language that you can communicate with Him, and He with you.

One of those stories is the book of Ruth. It is a beautiful story of covenant love. There is a special word in the Hebrew language that describes covenant love. It is *hesed.* It is usually translated *lovingkindness*, but that doesn't seem to do it justice. It speaks of the loyal, unbreakable bond of love that has committed itself selflessly to another. This special word is used three times in the book of Ruth.

The story begins as Naomi, her husband Elimelech, and her two sons move to the land of Moab during a famine. Elimelech dies in the land of Moab. While there, Naomi finds Moabite wives, Ruth and Orpah, for her sons. After about ten years, both of her sons die also. Her sons are childless, so Naomi has no husband and no heirs. Naomi decides to return to her homeland and urges her daughters-in-law to return to their families and find new husbands. She blesses them and says *"May the Lord deal kindly with you* (deal with *hesed*, covenant love), *as you have dealt with the dead and with me."* Orpah leaves, but Ruth covenants herself to her mother-in-law and promises never to leave her.

To understand the Jewish mindset, Naomi is severed from all hope. She has lost her land and her posterity. She has no son to carry on a name or inheritance, and no husband to produce a son. Think of it as a giant tree. It started with Abraham the seed of the entire tree. Every Jewish person realizes that Abraham is their father and the originator of the covenant with God. They are a special, holy people because of their lineage, because of Abraham.

The next, most important thing is their posterity. Continuing their line is important. Especially looking forward to Messiah, He is the end goal. They know they will produce Him. Naomi is like a severed branch. She has no way to continue her posterity. When a Jewish woman (or any woman) marries, she becomes a part of her husband's family line. He is dependent upon her to continue his family tree; she is dependent upon him to provide the seed. This is the cycle of posterity, and although it seems to be lost in our present culture, it was accepted and crucial in those days.

When they get to Bethlehem, it is barley harvest. Ruth goes out to the fields to glean, that is to pick what is left over after the harvest. She ends up in Boaz's field. He is a close relative of Elimelech. He shows favor to Ruth because of her kindness to Naomi. Boaz makes sure she is safe and gets extra food. She is even allowed to eat with the workers.

When Naomi finds out who offered this kindness to Ruth, she can see God's hand in this turn of events. She sees His *hesed* love, his covenant loyalty. She responds to Ruth *"May he (*Boaz*) be blessed of the Lord who (*the Lord*) has not withdrawn His kindness* (hesed, covenant loyalty and faithful love) *to the living and the dead. Again, Naomi said to her, 'The man is our relative, he is one of our **closest relatives**."* Ruth 2:20

The word closest relative is not a good translation. The Hebrew word is *goel* which is a kinsman redeemer. A kinsman redeemer was a close relative who could purchase back property lost by a family member. He could avenge a wrong. He was one who acts on behalf of a relative dead or alive. A kinsman redeemer must be a close relative, be willing, and able to purchase back what was lost by his relative. We also have the issue of a levirate marriage that we learned about with Tamar and Judah. A close relative was to raise up a seed for the dead relative. Naomi saw all this. Ruth may have seen a kind relative offering food, but Naomi knew God had seen her plight. She knew a baby was coming. She knew not only was God faithful to her, but also to her husband, Elimelech to raise up an heir for her dead husband and son!

After the harvest Naomi instructs Ruth to go to Boaz. When he lies down at the threshing floor, Ruth uncovers his feet and lays down beside them. Boaz awakens; he asks who is there.

Ruth responds *"I am Ruth, your maid. So spread your **covering** over your maid, for you are a **close relative** (a kinsman redeemer)."* Ruth 3:9 There are some hidden treasures in this verse also. The word for *covering* is *kanaph* it is literally *extremity or wings*. It is used in Ruth 2:12, Boaz says to Ruth *"May the Lord reward your work, and your wages be full from the Lord, the God of Israel, under whose **wings** you have taken refuge"*

The wings of the Jewish garment were the four corners of his outer cloak. On these he sewed four tassels or tzitziyot. This was commanded in Numbers 25:37-41 to help the Jewish people to remember to obey the commands of the Lord and be set apart to Him. These tassels also represent a person's authority.

199

The *Kanaph* or Wings in the Story of King Saul

We see the corner of the garment and what it represents several times in the life of King Saul. If you don't know the story of king Saul, here is a brief summary.

Israel demanded God that they have a king like the other nations. So, God told Samuel the prophet to anoint Saul as the first king of Israel. This seemed to take Saul totally by surprise. When Samuel was presenting Saul to the nation as their king, Saul went and hid among the baggage. At first it seemed Saul would be a good king, but twice he disobeyed God's direct commands, because he feared the people more than he feared God. The first time Saul did what only a priest was allowed to do; he offered a burnt offering, rather than wait for Samuel. The second incident was when Saul allowed the people to keep the spoils of war and also captured the king alive. God had specifically told Saul to destroy everything.

Because of this, God rejected him from being king and Samuel anointed David to be king of Israel. But although David was anointed king, he continued as a shepherd and then later as an assistant to Saul. David loved and respected Saul, but as David's popularity grew, Saul became jealous and tried to kill David. David had to flee and live as a fugitive.

At the time when King Saul disobeyed God, the prophet Samuel confronted his disobedience and then told him the Lord had rejected Saul from being King Saul in his dismay grabbed the *kanaph* (the edge, wings, extremity) of Samuel's garment and it tore off. Samuel used this as a prophetic act and told Saul *"The Lord has torn the kingdom from you today and has given it to your neighbor, who is better than you."* 1 Samuel 15:28

Later when Saul is pursuing David to kill him, Saul enters a cave to relieve himself. David and his men are hiding further back in the cave. David could have killed Saul, but he honors him as anointed by God. To prove to Saul that he did not want to hurt him, David simply cuts off the edge *(kanaph)* of Saul's garment. Even then his conscience bothered him. We don't know if David knew about Samuel's prophecy, but to Saul the message was loud and clear. Saul was not fighting David; he was fighting God. Here was David who was more righteous than he. He was holding the kanaph, the edge of his garment, the symbol of his kingdom in his hand. Saul responded, *"Now, behold, I know that you shall surely be king, and that the kingdom of Israel shall be established in your hand."* The corner of Saul's robe represented the kingdom and authority that he had lost through his disobedience. Can you get a picture of David holding up the edge of Saul garment in his hand? Did he realize the prophetic significance of what he was doing? I don't know. David was the anointed King of Israel who had not yet taken his throne. He was standing before the tragic figure of Saul, holding the symbol of his kingdom and authority, which Saul had lost through his disobedience. Now, God had given it into the hand of David. Now if you are picturing David standing there, superimpose Jesus, the Man. He is the King of all Kings and the Lord of all Lords, but He has not yet taken His throne. He is holding up the kanaph, the authority that Adam lost through his disobedience. He has all authority in His hand. He is saying *"All authority has been given to Me in heaven and on earth…"* Then what does He do with the kanaph? Like Boaz, He spreads it over you His bride. *"...go therefore …."* (Matt. 28:18-19a). Our King of kings will come and take the throne and rule not only heaven, but earth also. But until He does, He has covered us with His authority, and all of His victory is ours.

Back to Ruth, the edge of Boaz's garment had great significance and Boaz knew exactly what Ruth was asking. He answered her *"May you be blessed of the Lord, my daughter, you have shown your last **kindness** (hesed, covenant, loyal love) to be better than the first by not going after young men whether rich or poor."* (Ruth

3:10) What is Boaz saying here? Ruth's covenant devotion to her mother-in-law showed in her actions. She didn't desire to marry a younger man, but chose the kinsman redeemer and was able to redeem for Naomi her inheritance and raise up an heir for her husband and son's name. Ruth demonstrated true covenant love. I love this romantic moment of the vulnerable, Ruth, who was a Gentile and outside of the covenant, asking Boaz to cover her with his identity and graft Ruth and Naomi back into the inheritance of Israel. Boaz covers her with the edge of his garment! Boaz takes the necessary steps and secures the right to purchase the land and marry Ruth. Ruth 4:14 says "*The Lord enabled her* (Ruth) *to conceive and she gave birth to a son.*" I believe this was Naomi's faith and her blessing. "*The neighbor women gave him (the baby) a name saying 'a son has been born to Naomi…'*" This is what Naomi longed for: a child to carry on their family. The child born to Ruth was Obed who was the grandfather of King David. If you remember our chapter on *Following the Seed,* here is another act of faith that carried The Seed. Obed carried the Messiah, the Seed.

Of course, this is a beautiful type of Christ! He is the kinsman redeemer to Israel and to Adam! He will take back the earth, that Adam lost! He is the loving husband who spreads His identity over the church, allowing her to partake in all that He is! There is a reference to this in Revelation 7: 14-15. "*These are the ones who come out of the great tribulation, and they have washed their robes and made them white in the blood of the Lamb. For this reason, they are before the throne of God and they serve Him day and night in His temple and He who sits on the throne **will spread His tabernacle over them**.*" I see the tabernacle as a picture of who Jesus is and what He has done. He spreads this over us. This is who we are. I love how the Bible is like a photo album. There are hundreds of snapshots of Jesus and our Redemption!

Joshua The High Priest

Galatians 2:20 says *"I have been crucified with Christ; and it is no longer I who live, but Christ lives in me, and the life which I now live in the flesh, I live by faith in the Son of God, who loved me and gave Himself up for me."*

I hope those words, now, hold more meaning for you. They do for me. In closing this book, I would like to look back at one of those "snapshots" of Christ we looked at earlier. It is the passage in Zechariah about Joshua the high priest standing in the courtroom of heaven. This is a picture of Jesus the Man standing before the Lord. He is representing and carrying within Himself every "faith man" that is: every born-again believer. He is carrying us as Adam carried the human race and establishing our identity!

"Then he showed me Joshua (remember Joshua is the same name as Jesus just translated differently) *the high priest standing before the angel of the Lord, and Satan standing at his right hand to accuse him. The Lord said to Satan 'The Lord rebuke you, Satan! Indeed, the Lord who has chosen Jerusalem rebuke you! Is this not a **brand** plucked from the fire?"* (Zech. 3:1-2)

I had to look up what this meant. All I could think of was like a cattle brand. That is not what this means. It is an ember or piece of burned wood after a fire. It is what is left. So, God is rebuking Satan because Jesus the high priest has already gone through the fire of judgement. The price has already been paid. He is what is left after the fire! He and the race of born-again believers that He carries have been through judgement. The price has been paid. We are inside of Him, much in the same way Noah and his family were inside the ark! The judgement fell on Him. The price has been paid. There is nothing to accuse Him (or us!) of.

"Now Joshua was clothed with filthy garments and standing before the angel. He spoke and said to those

who were standing before him, saying, 'Remove the filthy garments from him.' Again, he said to him, 'See I have taken your iniquity away from you and will clothe you with festal robes.' "(Zech. 3:3-4)

This is our old man, our old identity, our sin, it is removed. Jesus the Man took the sin of the race of Adam. He as the head of the new race receives festal robes. We are clothed in His righteousness.

"Then I said, 'Let them put a clean turban on his head.' So, they put a clean turban on his head and clothed him with garments, while the angel of the Lord was standing by. And the angel of the Lord admonished Joshua saying, `Thus says the Lord of hosts, "If you will walk in My ways and if you will perform my service, then you will also govern My house and also have charge of My courts, and I will grant you free access among these who are standing here. Now listen, Joshua, the high priest, you and your friends who are sitting in front of you -indeed they are men who are a symbol, for behold I am going to bring in My servant the Branch."'"

At the end of the passage, the Bible even says Joshua is a symbol of Jesus. The Branch is referring to Jesus the Branch from the root of Jesse (King David's father). "If you will walk in My ways and if you perform My service, then you will also govern My house and also have charge of MY courts, and I will grant you free access among these who are standing here" Now there is no question in the verse about Jesus the high priest being faithful, but if we are faithful, we will have access to God's house, courts and angelic hosts!

Living in His Identity

In the first year of my marriage, my husband and I went off to school. After the school year was finished, we came home for a short visit before we were to spend the summer at a youth ranch. I went to the bank in our home town, not even thinking about the fact that I didn't have an account there anymore. I went to cash a check. In my mind it was still my bank. I presented my check to be cashed. The teller asked if I had an account there. I said no, I used to, but not anymore. She said," I am sorry, I can't cash your check."

I was really surprised. I thought they would cash my check. I panicked for a moment. I really needed to get this check cashed. Then I said "Would it help if I told you my dad is Lon DeNeff?"

"Oh, I am sorry, of course we can cash your check!" the teller apologized.

What changed? Well, you see, I thought about who my dad was. He was the manager of that bank! My identity could not get the check cashed, but my dad's identity could!

That is a picture of the Christian life! In our own identity, we just don't have the ability to do anything. But if we say… "Uh, would it help if I said my Lord is Jesus Christ?" Bam! That changes everything. You see, when we line our will with God's will and pray and say, "Uh, would it help if I tell you I am in Christ?"; it is the same as if Jesus prayed it. I have His identity! If sickness comes against you, first check and make sure you are submitted to God, then tell it to go, it is the same for you to get sick as it would be for Jesus to get sick. Can you picture Jesus getting sick? I can't. Of course, there is the other side of this too. If you are driving and someone cuts you off in traffic, uhm, I really don't think Jesus would lay on the horn (or worse).

I used to picture the Christian life in my head as this journey. I started at the cross, then I walked a little farther and was filled with the Spirit. I walked farther and got more understanding. You see, I thought that I was making progress. That pretty soon I would get to a place where I would be good enough for God to use me.

Now since understanding this, I live every moment in that first moment that I was born again, in that moment when I realized I was incapable of ever pleasing God and I needed Jesus. I live at the cross! Because it is there that I lose my identity and take on His! It is a place of death to myself, so that I can live in my Jesus suit. I am covered by His wings. Come on under with me, will you?

If you have never accepted Jesus, now is the best time. Would you like to pray with me?
Lord Jesus, I am not able to please God myself. I repent of my sin. I desire to be born of you. Thank you for becoming what I am, a human being. Thank you for taking the punishment for my sin and failure. I desire to be born of your seed. I give you my life.

I would encourage you to be baptized. You can go to a Bible believing church and be baptized, or any Christian can baptize you in any body of water. When you are, realize that something more is happening in the spirit realm. You are by faith entering in to Jesus, into His death, burial and resurrection! You are no longer the seed of Adam. You are the seed of Christ!

Made in the USA
Columbia, SC
30 December 2023

29658563R00124